just a boy

RICHARD McCANN

just a boy

The True Story
of a Stolen Childhood

EBURY
PRESS

This edition published in 2005
First published in Great Britain in 2004

10 9 8 7 6

Text © Richard McCann 2004

First published by
Ebury Press
Random House, 20 Vauxhall Bridge Road, London SW1V 2SA

Random House Australia (Pty) Limited
20 Alfred Street, Milsons Point, Sydney, New South Wales 2061, Australia

Random House New Zealand Limited
18 Poland Road, Glenfield, Auckland 10, New Zealand

Random House South Africa (Pty) Limited
Endulini, 5A Jubilee Road, Parktown 2193, South Africa

The Random House Group Limited Reg. No. 954009

www.randomhouse.co.uk

A CIP catalogue record for this book is available from the British Library.

Cover Design by Two Associates
Interior by seagulls

ISBN 0091898226

Printed and bound in Great Britain by Bookmarque Ltd, Croydon, Surrey

Papers used by Ebury Press are natural, recyclable products
made from wood grown in sustainable forests.

In loving memory of my mum, Williamina,
whose love has proved to be irreplaceable.

contents

acknowledgements

There are a number of people I would like to thank and the first has to be Andrew Beveridge, to whom I owe my life, Karen, a true friend in every sense, and Sandra Goad for helping me to deal with the issues of my childhood. Also Craig and Marion Shergould, who re-ignited my desire to write this book and Olga for her patience through the long phone calls. I would like to thank Pat and all at the Leeds Writers' Circle for pointing me in the right direction, not forgetting Michael Stewart. I would like to thank my agent, Judith Chilcote, for seeing the potential in what first dropped on her desk and for her ability to lift my spirits whenever they are down. I would like to mention all the teachers and friends I have made over the last few years on the salsa scene, they will all know who they are, and to Michael at Eagle Activity Tours. To Izaskuin, a small apology, she knows what for. Michiel in Watford, Jenny in Bradford, Jan and Bernice, Jill, Stewart, Steve and Pauline, Mushy and Emma, Nicoli and Helena and Samantha all deserve a mention for different reasons. A big thank you to my sister, Sonia, for her in-put into the story because it wouldn't have been the same without her. To Hannah and all the team at Ebury for making it happen, not forgetting Alex Hippisley Cox, my publicist, and lastly, a special thank you to Andrew Crofts for waving his magic wand over my work.

preface

Although this book is predominantly about my elder sister, Sonia, and me, what happened in our childhood caused as much pain and suffering to my other sisters. Twenty-five children were deprived of their mothers by Peter Sutcliffe, all of whom will understand how far reaching the effects of his actions have been. I believe that writing this book is already helping to heal some of the pain. I have often felt ashamed for the things that have happened around me, but realise now that they were not all my fault. I no longer have to be looking over my shoulder all the time, wondering what people do and do not know about my past.

I know that our father will be hurt by some of the facts in this book but I am convinced that our story needs to be told, to be out in the open. I have forgiven him for the way he brought us up and the writing of the book has helped us to begin to bridge the gap between us.

Children are precious and we must all help them whenever we see they need protection in order to turn them into stable adults. We all need to learn to put others before ourselves and to forgive rather than to carry grudges. I feel that in writing this book and discovering these things I am no longer just a boy.

chapter one
the morning after

Leeds, October 1975

I didn't want to wake up, but my sister Sonia was shaking me urgently.

'Mum's still not home,' she whispered, trying not to disturb the others.

I slept in one bed with Sonia and our younger sister Donna. Angela, the baby, was in a cot next to us, and had cried all night. She always seemed to be crying. Mostly I liked sharing with the girls because it helped us to keep warm. There was no heating of any kind in the house, and when we went to sleep we huddled under two or three blankets and any coats we could find. The only drawback to sharing was that when one of us wet the bed – which happened quite frequently – we all got soaked.

The previous evening Mum had sent us upstairs early. A few minutes after seven we heard her taking a bath then going downstairs. Sonia sneaked down after her. Mum, she told me, was in her white trousers and green jacket, and doing her make-up in a piece of broken mirror, salvaged from one of her many fights with her boyfriend and propped up above the square pot sink in the kitchen.

'Are you going out, Mum?' Sonia had asked.

'No, I'm not. You get back to bed. Go on.'

But Sonia knew she was on her way out and had asked for a kiss.

'Come on then, before I put my lipstick on.'

As she kissed her on the lips, Sonia noticed how nice and clean she smelled, a mixture of soap and perfume.

Hours later, in the middle of the night, when no one came to answer Angela's screams, Sonia ventured downstairs again. The house was silent and empty.

Sonia had taken charge of the situation as she always did. She had turned the bedroom light on and read to Angela to calm her down. I had drifted off to the sound of her voice.

There was never any predicting what time our mother would roll in, or what state she would be in when she got there, but we normally had a babysitter, and Mum was always there by the time we woke up in the morning, even if she could barely drag herself out of bed.

'What time is it?' I asked Sonia now.

'Twenty-five past five.'

'What shall we do?'

'Get up. We'll go and look for her.'

I always did what Sonia said – she was seven and a year older than me – so I pulled myself out of the warm bed. There was ice on the inside of the little bedroom window that looked out over the back garden and the bare floorboards were freezing. We crept downstairs, leaving Donna and Angela asleep upstairs. I put my brown duffel coat on over my green checked pyjamas and pulled my shoes on without socks, which felt strange. Sonia was wearing a coat over her full-length purple nightdress. She was taller than me, with long brown hair and fine features.

The kitchen was still strewn with the remnants of the supper Mum had made before her night out. She always cooked an evening meal for us, no matter how short of money she was. We let ourselves out through the back door, pulling it to behind us. Mum preferred us to go out this way, rather than through the front door, with everyone watching.

My heart was thumping in my chest. It was still dark outside and the normally familiar garden was silent and filled with threatening shadows. I remember the grass was wet on my bare ankles. Usually, if we were out the back we would have been able to hear raised voices from the neighbouring houses, radios and televisions playing through open windows and shouts from the Prince Philip playing fields behind the house. But everyone else was still asleep. We pushed our way through the hole in the hedge that we always used.

The Scott Hall council estate, which had always been my home, was about two miles north of the centre of Leeds, a sprawling mass of streets lined with redbrick houses and connected by a network of ginnels or alleys. It had been built just before the war and every house was pretty much identical. We lived at 65 Scott Hall Avenue, which was the end house in a block of four.

We walked along the path at the back of the house, close to the hedge like Mum had taught us, so that none of the neighbours could see us and gossip about what we were up to. But there wasn't anyone around at that hour anyway. There was a mist covering the ground and in the darkness we couldn't see more than a few feet in front of ourselves.

I kept asking Sonia questions, desperate for her to put my mind at rest. I wanted her to tell me where we were going, where Mum was.

'She's probably just gone to the shops for cigs or milk,' she said, but it seemed a funny time of the day to be shopping, even for Mum.

We soon reached a gateway that led back to our street. We hurried across the street and into the ginnel that ran past the houses opposite and out to the main dual carriageway. I kept expecting to see Mum coming in the other direction. Usually the traffic would be streaming past, but this morning there was only the odd car, headlights reflecting off the wet surface of the road, as people set off early for work, or came back from night shifts. A milk float jangled past.

'We'll wait at the bus stop,' Sonia told me, 'and meet her off the bus. She's bound to be back soon.'

I did as she instructed, sitting down beside her on the seat of the shelter, my feet swinging. It was cold around the bottoms of my legs. A double-decker bus appeared at the far end of the road after a few moments and, as we watched it approach with its brightly-lit interior, my heart lifted. I was sure she would be on it. She would probably scold us for coming out of the house on our own, but it would be worth it to be able to walk back home with her and climb into a warm bed. The bus driver indicated that he was drawing in at the stop and the doors hissed open. No one got off.

'You getting on then?' he called out to us.

'No,' Sonia shook her head. 'We're waiting for our mum.'

The man muttered something under his breath, the doors slapped shut again and the bus drew away.

'She'll probably be on the next one,' Sonia reassured me. 'Don't worry.'

As the sky became lighter, the frequency of the buses drawing up at the stop increased, but Mum still didn't get off any of them. After we'd been there an hour and seen ten buses come and go, Sonia began to fret that Donna and Angela would have woken up at home and would be wondering where we were.

We decided to make our way back. The houses that had been dark when we set out were now full of light as people woke and got ready for the day. I hoped nobody would look out and see us because I knew Mum would be angry with us for coming downstairs and leaving the house without her. She was quite strict about that sort of thing.

I wondered if Mum might be waiting inside for us, her arms folded, demanding to know what we were playing at. It would have been a relief to see her, because we were beginning to feel really scared, but at the same time I didn't want to get into trouble.

'Go upstairs and see if she's in the bedroom or the bathroom,' Sonia instructed when we got in. She checked the rest of the house.

It didn't take long for us to exhaust the possibilities in our small home.

'What should we do?' I asked, frightened but sure Sonia would know the answers.

'I'll go and get Angela and Donna up,' she said, trying to sound certain.

I got dressed and went down to the kitchen to prepare us all some cereal. I put out the bowls and mixed up some powdered milk. We often didn't have the money to buy fresh milk, although there always seemed to be hundreds of empty bottles all round the kitchen, their dregs turning to cream and giving off a sour smell.

'Should we go to school?' I asked when Sonia came in with the little ones. Some mornings, after her nights out, Mum wouldn't be able to wake up and we'd have to walk ourselves to school. It was too far for such small children really, but Sonia and I thought we were grown up enough to do it.

'I don't know,' Sonia admitted, settling Angela in her high chair. 'Let's just get ready.'

All four of us sat down to breakfast at the table as if nothing unusual was happening. When we finished eating, Sonia obviously wasn't sure what we should do next. She and I should be going to school, but we could hardly leave Donna and Angela on their own. It looked as if we might have to go in late.

'Go to the front gate, Richard, and see if she's coming up the street,' Sonia said.

I did as I was told. It was light now and I could see that there was some sort of commotion going on at the end of Scott Hall Avenue. A couple of police cars were parked there, and their flashing blue lights were attracting a crowd of onlookers, just a few yards from the route Sonia and I had walked earlier. It was unusual to see police cars around at that time in the morning; they usually came out at night to answer complaints or break up domestic quarrels. I went back in and told Sonia that something was happening in the street.

'Stay here and play with Angela for a moment,' she told Donna as she put the baby down on the sofa. 'Richard and I will see what's going on outside.'

Some instinct told me that the scene we were walking towards had something to do with us. I felt nervous without knowing why. As we got nearer, I recognised two neighbours who were talking to policemen. One officer spotted us and came over.

'And who might you two be?' he asked.

'Sonia and Richard McCann,' Sonia told him.

'And where are you off to?'

'Our mum hasn't come home,' I said. 'We're looking for her.'

Very suddenly, the policeman looked concerned. 'Where do you live?' he asked, and we told him.

He said something into his radio and then walked us back to the front door. We let ourselves back in and he followed us. I think the house was probably a bit of a tip. Mum was never great at the housework. He started asking us lots of questions as the four of us sat huddled together on the sofa.

'Where's your dad?'

'He doesn't live with us,' Sonia explained. I was proud of the way she spoke up.

'When did you last see your mum?'

'Last night.'

'Are you all brothers and sisters?'

Sonia nodded.

'Do you have a photograph of your mum?' he asked.

'All our photographs were burned,' Sonia said. I didn't know about that, but I'd never seen any photos around the house and burning them was something that Mum's boyfriend, Keith, might very easily have done in one of his tempers.

The policeman went out into the kitchen to use his radio again. We could hear his voice and the crackle of the responses, but I couldn't make out what he was saying. Sonia was looking pale. When the man came back into the room he seemed uncomfortable and unsure what to say to us. Sonia got up and turned on the television to cover the awkwardness of the moment. We all pretended to watch it with our full attention, even the policeman, so we didn't have to talk.

After a while another policeman arrived, in plain clothes this time. He introduced himself and said he was going to look after us. He was talking very softly, like he was our uncle or something, very friendly, even though we didn't know him. He asked us all to come out to the police car that was waiting outside. We didn't often get to travel in cars. I knew that Mum must be in some sort of trouble.

All four of us climbed into the back seat and we were driven slowly away from Scott Hall Avenue. None of us had any idea where we were going. I caught Sonia's eye and I knew now that she was as frightened and disorientated as I was. We just wanted the fuss to stop and for Mum to come home.

The journey lasted about ten minutes before we turned into what looked like a long street lined with terraced houses. At the end, tucked well away from passers-by, was a narrow opening that led to a slightly wooded area. A thin gravel path wound through the trees and the police car crunched slowly along it until it reached a large, grey-brick Victorian building. A sign announced this was Beckett's Park Children's Home. It looked more like an abbey, two storeys high and as wide as four normal houses. Steps led up to imposing double doors. Although I was nervous about what was happening, all the attention was now making me feel quite special. I remember thinking that it was actually quite nice to be away from the usual shouting at home.

As we came in with the policeman, the staff seemed to be expecting us. We were given cups of hot chocolate and taken to a room with a television. After a while, once we were settled in comfortably, the policeman came back in to see us. He felt more like a friend by now. He sat down and said he had something to tell us.

'Your mum has been taken to heaven,' he said. 'You won't be seeing her any more.'

Someone had attacked our mum, without warning or explanation, the policeman said. His words seemed jumbled, unreal. I needed time to sort them out and think about them. Such a terrible thing couldn't really happen, could it? It just didn't make sense. I relied on Mum completely, how was it possible that she was no longer there for me? It wasn't possible, I decided eventually. The policeman had made a mistake and she would be coming back one way or another. I stopped listening to him. If she could be taken away to heaven so easily, I was sure she could be returned. I simply had to wish hard enough and everything would be normal again.

The next few hours crawled past us as we sat, numb and dazed, while life at Beckett's Park went on around us.

Everything was unfamiliar; we didn't know the routines of the home or where we would be sleeping that night. We had no idea what was going to be happening to us in an hour's time, let alone what the next days, weeks or years held in store. We moved from one moment to the next that day, from sitting in a silent row on the sofa to another room where we were given meals. We made trips to the loo and just existed, waiting to be told what to do. We didn't talk to each other and nobody explained what was going on.

Out of our sight, however, phone calls were made and discussions were held – and after being given dinner we were asked to go to the visitors' room. I hoped this meant Mum had come back down from heaven to see us. The room was full of toys and we were sat down on a sofa and each given something to hold. I think I had a train. Whatever it was I sat holding it while a photographer came in and took some pictures. Our bewildered and glum little faces would soon be all over the national papers.

I didn't like the way no one was saying anything about Mum. It was as if she'd never existed.

But no one at Beckett's Park Children's Home wanted to talk about how two small children had walked just yards away from their mother's murdered body, only saved from finding her by the early morning mist.

chapter two

he's our dad

The hours turned into long, drawn-out days and the pain refused to subside. I just wanted to sit and stare out of the window, struggling to sort my thoughts and feelings and to remember all the times I'd had with Mum and the things she used to say and do. If I could picture her clearly enough in my imagination then it felt almost as if she was still there.

'You see the stars up there?' a staff member said one night, directing my attention up into the night sky.

'Yes,' I said.

'Look for the brightest one you can find, because that one is your mum, watching over you all.'

I stared up at the stars for a long time, trying to find the brightest one, but they looked awfully far away and I wanted her to be there in the room with me, so that I could cuddle her and tell her about how frightened I was and how much I loved her and to hear her reassurances that everything would be all right. The unhappiness sometimes seemed too heavy to bear and my chest felt as though it would cave in under the pressure of my misery. I wanted so much to release the pain and to be able to breathe freely again, but there didn't seem to be any way of doing it as long as Mum wasn't there, and it was beginning to dawn on me that now she never would be there, that I was going to have to find a way to cope without her.

Mum had lived in Leeds since she was seventeen, having followed her brothers south from Inverness. She was the sixth child in a family of eleven and her full name was Willliamina, although everyone called her Wilma. She always made everyone laugh. Men liked Mum, except Dad and her boyfriends, of course. She dyed her strawberry blonde hair herself, but never bothered to wear protective gloves for the job, so although her hair looked wonderful, usually pulled up on top of her head, her hands were always red and raw-looking from the bleach. I inherited my thick ginger hair from her side of the family as well as my green eyes and, so I was told, huge amounts of energy.

Our uncles used to come to stay quite often, bringing a bit of extra money into the house. The one who stayed the most was Raymond. He taught us how to turn two-pence pieces into ten-pence pieces by covering them with a film of silver paper from inside cigarette packets and rubbing them on our foreheads until the Queen's head showed through. It worked and meant we had more money to spend on sweets, so long as the man in the shop didn't look too closely.

Our dad, Gerry McCann, had also come to Leeds in search of a better life. He was a joiner from Londonderry in Northern Ireland. They had us four kids before he and Mum split up. There were often violent rows and once or twice Mum ended up being admitted to a psychiatric ward as a result.

She liked to be out most weekends, and recently her weekends had begun on Thursdays. She used to go down to the city centre every Saturday as well. She told us it was to do some shopping, but from the way she applied her make-up and back-combed her hair, Sonia and I guessed she popped into a pub or two along the way. She would leave Sonia 50p to buy us sweets and ice creams.

Then on Sundays, which were bath nights, Mum would get out the nit comb. She was always very rough with it, reducing poor Donna, who had a mass of thick, brown hair, to tears.

'There are women who would give their right arms to have hair as thick as yours, Donna,' she used to say. 'You'll be glad of it one day.'

Sonia always told me I was Mum's favourite, mainly because I was a boy I suppose. She certainly took a lot more cheek from me than she did from the others. As I stared out of the window at Beckett's Park, I remembered an incident when I was sent up to bed before I'd finished eating – I'd been messing around at the table – and I had stamped upstairs angrily and run into my bedroom. We couldn't afford carpets, and Mum had cleaned the lino that afternoon. My feet skidded out from under me, pitching me headfirst into the metal bedpost with the force of a small missile. I didn't feel any pain for a moment, but I knew it was serious from the amount of blood streaming down my face.

I remembered sitting on Mum's knee in the local hospital waiting for the doctor to see me. It was just the two of us and I felt very close to her. I didn't care about the cut any more because I was able to cuddle her as much as I wanted and she wasn't going anywhere.

She was also ferociously protective of all of us. I was an inquisitive child and would wander out of the house at every opportunity, so Mum was forever sending poor Sonia out to look for me. When I was about four I decided to explore the playing fields, even though Mum had told me not to go beyond the bottom half of Scott Hall Avenue. The moment I stepped over the invisible boundary line I found myself surrounded by a gang of older boys. I immediately sensed that I was in trouble.

'Take your trousers down,' one of them said, and the others sniggered.

I told them I didn't want to, but they weren't going to let me get out of it, and eventually I pulled my trousers down to my ankles, hoping that then they would leave me alone. It felt very humiliating and frightening.

'Get on your hands and knees,' they said then, and they began to push grass up my bottom. It wasn't terribly painful but it was a terrible invasion and I didn't know if or when they were going to stop. Tears were pouring down my cheeks as they ran off, laughing, leaving me to pull my trousers back up and run home.

Mum made me tell her what had happened to get me in such a state. She was angry with me for disobeying her and going so far from the house, but she was furious with the other kids. She dragged me straight back out to the playing fields. I pointed out the gang and she stormed over to them, demanding to know who they were and where they lived. Then she went round to have a word with the ringleader's parents. When Mum 'had a word' with you in her broad Scottish accent you knew all about it. She was what you might call a feisty woman. She wasn't scared of anyone.

Keith, who came to live with us once Dad had gone, used to argue with Mum just as badly as Dad had. He was a stocky man with curly brown hair and a mouth full of shiny white teeth. She was always careful to get us all upstairs when the trouble started. But we could see the black eyes and bust lips on her the next day. It was almost worse for Sonia, Donna, Angela and me to sit upstairs on the bed, crying and trying to cover our ears, as we listened to them shouting and screaming and the crash of things being broken downstairs. As soon as we heard the front door slam we'd know that Keith had stormed out again and we'd sneak downstairs to see if she was all right.

To many people it was a troubled childhood, but it didn't

seem that bad to me. It was all I'd ever known and many of the families around us on the estate lived similar lives. Everyone was short of money, everyone fought and argued and did the best they could to get by. Violence and poverty were the norm; women got beaten and men drank too much. We all wore hand-me-down clothes from the charity shops and nobody ever had any spare cash for anything but drink and cigarettes.

Although we were poor, Mum always had lots of ideas of how to make a few bob, or scam a little here and there. Whenever there was a knock on the door that she reckoned might mean someone was round to collect money, she would have us all hidden behind the sofa within seconds. She taught us how to make flowers out of coloured crêpe paper and would then send us out to knock on doors and sell our wares. I suppose it was begging really, but we didn't have much success. She had another trick of making little baskets out of oranges by slicing out two segments to make a handle and then scooping out the rest. I never knew what to do with the baskets, but I enjoyed making them. I also used to earn a few pence by going to the shop for an old lady called Betty, who lived alone next door. I liked listening to her stories about the war and how she'd been hit by shrapnel. My favourite scam was saving Green Shield stamps to trade for packets of biscuits, and cigarette cards that you could take back for money.

* * *

On the second day at Beckett's Park, we were taken back into the visitors' room. A man walked in with a member of staff and sat down at a small table, watching us. He looked familiar but I couldn't place him.

'Do you know this man?' the staff member asked Sonia.

'Yes,' she replied, 'he's our dad.'

Even though he'd only left Mum eighteen months previously, I didn't recognise him. He was a stranger to us. I didn't feel any sort of connection to this man who sat there silently, watching us play. He didn't stay long, but promised to visit us again soon.

The last time I'd seen him was a year before, when he turned up unexpectedly at the house to see us one evening, knocking on the back door. Keith was there at the time and from the other room we could hear the two men shouting angrily at one another in the kitchen. Then Dad had barged his way through to the living room. Keith came after him with a hammer, shouting aggressively. Sonia and I were in our nightclothes, ready for bed, and Dad lifted us up, carrying us to the door, one under each arm, and taking us to a taxi that was waiting outside the house with its engine running.

He took us to his older sister, Katherine, whose house was on the other side of Leeds. Katherine had a proper family home with a husband, Alan (who was bald), and three children, Melanie, Damian and Patrick (who were all older than us). Their house was nice, a great deal warmer and more comfortable than ours, and we got to borrow our cousins' clothes, which made me feel much smarter than usual, but a bit ashamed. They had what seemed like hundreds of brass and copper plates on the walls of the living room and the walls were lined with wooden panels. They even had a colour television with a radio on it. Our cousins had nicely decorated bedrooms and there were always delicious meals on the table for them. I would have loved to live in a home like that.

The next day Mum came round to Katherine's in tears and begged Dad to let us come home, which he agreed to so easily I couldn't really understand why he'd taken us in the first place. Maybe he just didn't like having Keith telling him what to do with his own children, or maybe he just wanted to make a point. I would quite like to have stayed in Auntie Katherine's nice comfortable house, but Sonia said we should go back because Mum needed looking after.

At Christmas that year Dad left presents for all four of us in the living room when Keith was out. He hadn't bothered to wrap them so we could see what they were. There was a large yellow Tonka truck for me, two panda bears as tall as Sonia for Angela and Donna, and a similar-sized doll for Sonia. We were all very excited by their arrival; I had never in my life had anything as wonderful as that truck. The previous Christmas Mum had taken us to the Social Services and we had been allowed to choose one toy each. I'd chosen a wooden fort, which I had really liked, but this truck was even better.

'Where have these come from?' Keith roared at Mum when he got home and discovered the presents.

'Gerry,' she replied.

He was angry, partly at discovering Dad had been in the house when Mum was alone, and partly because he knew he couldn't afford to buy us anything for Christmas himself. As always, Mum hurried us upstairs and we sat on the edge of the bed, listening to the screaming and thumping from below. We were used to hearing Keith attacking her, but this time it sounded as if she was giving as good as she got. We sat, silent and shivering, until we heard the inevitable slam of the front door.

Eventually we plucked up the courage and made our way down. As we reached the bottom of the stairs we could hear the horrible sound of our mother sobbing. Sonia gingerly pushed the living-room door open and revealed Mum on the far edge of the sofa, next to the fire, desperately trying to push the stuffing back into one of the panda bears. Both the bears had been ripped to pieces and the doll lay naked and limbless on the floor. My Tonka truck had been smashed to pieces.

Mum said I could play with what was left and I sat on the floor with a few wheels, imagining I had the whole truck, while Mum sat on the sofa for the rest of the evening, trying to sew the bears back together. Keith didn't return that night and we secretly hoped that Mum wouldn't let him back into the house after that, but she did. He came back the following night, his arms full of chocolates for her and tangerines for us. Mum never said a word, just kept on sewing one of the pandas without looking up. Then she offered Sonia a chocolate, which triggered another argument, and we were back on our way upstairs.

'I bought them for you,' he was shouting at her as we left the room.

She had a new black eye the next morning.

Someone obviously made the decision that we weren't yet able to cope with going back to school, but a few days after we arrived at the home some of our teachers came to visit us, bringing work for us to do. It was a strange feeling to see familiar faces from our former lives coming into a place where everyone and everything was new to us. They were obviously ill at ease, unsure what to say and how to act.

At the end of the week Sonia spent an afternoon on her own with the police. They took her round the shops in Leeds to look for a purse similar to the one Mum had taken out the night she went to heaven and which had disappeared. They wanted to use it as a clue in the search for Mum's killer. Sonia wasn't able to find one exactly like it, but she grew bored with looking and in the end just chose one that was similar and told them it was the one. She then wrote 'MUMIY' inside it, just as one of us had done with the original purse.

Many years later I met a policeman who worked on what became known as the hunt for the Yorkshire Ripper, and he told me that for many years he kept a police bulletin of that one word on the wall above his desk as a reminder of what that man had done to our family that night.

The following week they decided we were sufficiently recovered to be able to face school once more. We were to be ferried back and forth by taxi, something that we'd only ever done as a special treat before, which made us feel very important. One morning the taxi driver took us to the wrong school by mistake and drove up Scott Hall Avenue, painfully reminding us that we would never be able to go back to our life as it was.

No one ever mentioned Mum at school but there was an obvious change in everyone's attitudes towards us. I have to admit I did take advantage of the teachers' kindness from time to time, pretending to be ill in order to get taken to the sickbay, where I could lie down in peace for hours with my own thoughts and have the teachers popping in and out every few minutes to see if I was all right. I loved the feeling of being the centre of attention, of having someone care for me just like Mum had.

There was a tradition at the school Christmas party for one lucky child to find a sixpence inside his or her portion of Christmas cake. I don't know if I really was lucky that year or if someone had made sure that 'poor little Richard' got the money. I didn't care. I was just happy to be the one to get the magical coin.

Dad started to visit us most weekends, taking us out to a children's matinée at the local cinema on Saturday afternoons. I'd never been to a cinema before and I loved it. It made me feel like we were normal children, doing normal family things with our dad. But he couldn't always be relied upon to come when he promised. Sometimes we would sit in the visitors' room, staring out of the window at the gravel path that he should have been walking up at any moment. We'd see other parents arriving and then leaving with their kids, the house growing more and more silent around us as the minutes ticked by. We would begin to feel embarrassed and foolish and eventually would have to admit to ourselves that he wasn't coming and go back to our bedroom to pass the time as best we could. Although we always felt upset and disappointed when he let us down, we were sure he must have good reasons for not being able to get to us and realised that we were an inconvenience to him. He had been forced to be our dad again by circumstances. He didn't owe us anything.

One weekend he took us to visit his new girlfriend, Pauline, at the little terraced house they were living in. Pauline was only twenty-one years old and prettier than Mum had been. She was also heavily pregnant, which was another reason Mum had been so unhappy, and Dad told us the baby was due any day.

'We're going to sell this house,' he told us on one visit. 'And get the council to find one big enough for us all to live in together.'

I didn't get my hopes up, knowing that he didn't always keep his promises, but as the days turned into weeks I did begin to imagine how nice it would be if we could all live together as a family in a normal house, even if Pauline wasn't our real mum.

'Your dad rang,' a staff member told us a few days later. 'He asked us to tell you that Pauline has gone into hospital and had a baby girl. They're going to call her Cheryl. Isn't that good news?'

It was obvious they expected us to be pleased and since Sonia seemed to be happy I thought I'd better pretend I was as well, but I wasn't. Why should I care about this baby? Pauline wasn't my mum, I reasoned, so Cheryl wasn't going to be my sister.

Dad actually did come through on his promise to get the council to find a home for us all, seven weeks after we arrived at Beckett's Park. Just before we were all due to leave the home and move into the new house, it was arranged for Sonia and me to spend a weekend with a foster family who took us away to a caravan site. They probably thought it would be a nice holiday for us. The staff never told us that Donna and Angela were going to be looked after by someone else, or explained where they had gone. I guess they thought it didn't matter but it worried us because we couldn't understand why we'd been split up. Sonia and I got very nervous whenever we were separated from each other. The authorities were good about recognising that because lots of people were reading about us in the papers and offering to foster us, but no one wanted all four of us and so we stayed at the home until Dad was able to take us.

It rained all the time that weekend in the caravan and both of us wet our beds. We were told to wash our own sheets by hand in the sink as a punishment, which made us feel very ashamed.

Our new home was on a long sloping road called Broadlea Street, in Bramley. It was very similar to Scott Hall Avenue, with about eighty houses on each side of the road. The living room faced out towards the street and a big tree in the front garden blocked out all the sunlight, making the room gloomy and unwelcoming. It had none of the warmth or comfort of Auntie Katherine's house, but it was a new beginning and I thought that now everything was going to be all right.

From the window of the bedroom that was going to be ours I could see the tall white tower of Leeds University. I'd been able to see the same tower from the window at Scott Hall Avenue. It seemed like a connecting point to our previous life and in the coming years I would spend hours just staring at it and dreaming of how things used to be.

For the first few nights Dad looked after us on his own, while we waited for Pauline and Cheryl to join us. We all slept in the same bed, and I felt very secure as I lay there, watching the red glow of his cigarette end dancing in the dark like a firefly.

I thought I knew now why Mum had been taken away from us: she had been a sacrifice so that we could have a better life with our father.

chapter three

a new 'Mum'

I still had no idea what had happened on the night Mum had gone to heaven, but no one would discuss it, least of all Dad, so I was left alone with my imagination. I'm sure everyone was trying to spare my feelings, but I wanted to talk about Mum all the time. I was desperate to understand it. Even Sonia and I avoided the subject when we were alone, in case Dad caught us whispering. He was the adult, we reasoned, so he must know best. If he didn't want the subject talked about then we must leave it buried. But I do remember one instance when he brought a friend home and showed him some newspaper cuttings about Mum. The man gave us a pound to share on sweets, which went quite a long way in those days.

No one told us anything about Mum's funeral. We certainly weren't expected to attend. We didn't know when it was held, nor did we know where she was being put to rest. She just disappeared on that October night and that was the last we knew about her.

Mum's brother Isaac and his wife Vicky started coming to visit us, and would invite us back to their house at weekends. It was only a couple of miles away and they were always very kind and caring towards us.

'Who's this then?' Auntie Vicky would ask, pointing to a small oval photo which hung in her hallway in a frame about the size of an egg. We knew it was Mum, even though the tiny grainy picture bore no resemblance to the woman we remembered. 'Don't you ever forget her, will you?'

I had no intention of ever doing such a thing. Reminders of Mum seemed to be everywhere. If *The Flintstones* came on the television we would turn over, not wanting to hear Fred Flintstone shouting 'Wilma' over and over again. There was also a song out at the time which I kept hearing everywhere and which seemed to be taunting me: 'I woke up this morning and my mother was gone'. Then came the chorus, over and over again: 'Where's your mama gone? Where's your mama gone? Far, far away ...'

Dad soon began to show us that he was going to be strict. Where Mum used to send us up to the bedroom if we were misbehaving or being cheeky, Dad would threaten to send us back to Beckett's Park if we displeased him in any way. Whenever he issued the threat I would burst into tears. They weren't real tears but I thought if I could let him see that he had succeeded in frightening me, then he wouldn't need to resort to more drastic punishments. At that stage he had never hit us, but I got the feeling he easily could do if he was at all provoked.

Everyone else liked Dad. Whenever he was in company he was always the one cracking the jokes and making people laugh. Everyone wanted to have him around because he was such good company and we were constantly told how lucky we were to have such a good bloke for a dad. But he didn't seem such a great bloke when he was at home; he certainly wasn't much of a home-maker for the family. We got the bare essentials in the way of furniture but Dad never did anything about cheering the place up or making it feel more homely. In our bedrooms the paint-work remained cracked and peeling, there was no wallpaper and everything looked worn-out.

It seemed odd when Pauline and Cheryl moved in with us, because although she was the mother figure of the family, she wasn't Mum. It was only two months since Mum had gone and already it seemed as if she'd been replaced, as if she'd never existed, as if we were supposed to forget all about her and just carry on with the new model. But at least the four of us were together and we had a home and someone looking after us. Things could have been worse, at least that's what Sonia and I kept telling each other. However difficult it was for us, it must have been equally difficult for Pauline, a twenty-one-year-old girl, who suddenly had five children to look after, four of whom were deeply scarred by losing their mother in such a sudden and brutal way.

We were enrolled at a new school, five minutes' walk from the house. Auntie Pauline, as we had been told to call her, walked me there on the first day, taking me in to meet my new teacher in Class Seven. She was a lovely woman called Miss Carr. She was slim and dark-haired and made me feel very welcome. Despite Miss Carr's kindness, I still felt like an outsider because all the other children looked normal and I felt different. I didn't know exactly what 'normal' was, but I knew no one else in that classroom had been through what I'd been through.

I have no good memories about those early months in our new home, but no terrible ones either. We just continued living from day to day, hoping that things would settle and we would start to feel better about life.

The only heating at Broadlea Street was a small gas fire in the living room, so the bedrooms were always ice cold. At bedtime Dad would fill empty pop bottles from the kettle and place them between the sheets to take some of the chill off, but they only ever warmed up small patches amidst the chilly expanses. Because it was some time before we had enough beds for all of us, we still had to share with one another. Sonia and I invented a game in which we would stroke and tickle one another's backs. We would give each other fifty 'credits', which we could spend on different kinds of strokes. It was the closest both of us came to receiving physical affection from anyone. I used to pretend to fall asleep while Sonia was stroking my back, hoping she would continue, even after I had run out of credit. She often did.

Soon, Pauline asked us to call her 'Mum' and Dad backed her up. It didn't seem right to us, but if that was what Dad wanted, then we would do it. It was surprising how quickly using the name became a habit, especially once Cheryl started to talk, but it still felt like a betrayal whenever I did it.

About three months after Mum had been taken from us, an article appeared in the *Yorkshire Post* about another woman who'd been murdered. Her name was Emily Jackson and she had two children. In a perverse way it somehow comforted me to know that we weren't alone, that somewhere out there other children were having the same experience as us, making us just slightly less different from the rest of the world.

Emily's body had also been found in Leeds, not far from Scott Hall Avenue. Many years later I discovered that she was actually found on the day that Mum was buried. The newspaper article linked the two deaths together and suggested they might have been committed by the same person, even though there was very little evidence to support this theory at that point.

Someone then made a television programme about the two murders, which contained reconstructions of both. For the first time it seemed we might actually find out what had happened to Mum on the night she died. I remember standing outside our house talking to Gary Dudley, a boy who lived next door. The Dudleys seemed to have everything that we didn't, especially a mum who was lots of fun. She would make them cups of tea when we were visiting, something we would never get at home, and I couldn't believe that any children were allowed to drink something so grown up. We were joined that day by another neighbour, Malcolm, a man of around forty who lived alone and liked to spend his time at his gate, watching the world go by and chatting to anyone who cared to stop for long enough to listen. Malcolm began to tell us about the reconstruction, which he'd watched the night before, and my stomach started to churn as his words triggered pictures in my head. I listened in silence as he and Gary chatted about the actress who had been impersonating my mum in the hope that it would jog someone's memory about what might have happened that night. It certainly jogged my memory, reminding me of that October morning and what Mum must have been going through while we were fast asleep. I couldn't believe that an adult felt it was all right to talk about such things in front of me, but at the same time I thought that adults always knew best, so I remained silent and dry-eyed.

My imagination began to take the few facts and scraps of information that I'd been able to glean about Mum's murder, and was juggling them around in my head. I started to think that there was someone out there who was going to kill me as well, given the opportunity. I didn't tell anyone about my fears, but they were growing with every day that passed and I did my best never to be alone anywhere.

The summer of 1976 was one of the hottest on record and when Dad cut down the tree in the front garden the sunshine came streaming in through the windows, brightening up the atmosphere but making the shabbiness of the rooms even more noticeable. We used to take family outings to the local canal, walking along the banks for a couple of miles, carrying a picnic lunch. We would pass two locks and at the third one there was a large, flat, grassy area where families used to lay out their picnics. You had to get there early to get the best positions. We'd lie in the sun or play football or throw a Frisbee back and forth. Sometimes Malcolm from next door would tag along. He and Dad were becoming quite friendly.

Not far from the canal there was a disused quarry where Dad thought he might be able to scrounge some discarded timber. He had a plan to build a shed because he wanted to keep greyhounds for racing, a family tradition apparently. Dad suggested that he and Malcolm and I went on to the quarry after one of these afternoon picnics to see what we could find.

I liked the idea of being included in such an interesting mission but when we got to the woods on the rim of the quarry and looked down the steep sides Dad had second thoughts as to whether it would be safe for me to go down.

'You wait here,' he told me. 'Malcolm and I will go down for the wood.'

I agreed quite happily and it wasn't until the two men had disappeared out of sight below me and I could no longer hear their voices or the sound of their footsteps, that I realised I was all alone on the edge of the woods with dusk approaching. I'd got myself into exactly the sort of position I most feared. What if someone came along? What was to stop them murdering me? I was convinced that the killer who was out to get me would be appearing from the early evening shadows of the trees at any moment. Every rustle and movement in the leaves seemed to announce his arrival. Maybe the person who had killed Mum had been watching our house and was just waiting for an opportunity to get me on my own in a deserted spot. Fear swept through me and I started to scream hysterically at the top of my voice. Then I thought that if my killer was close and heard me scream he would have to act quickly in order to shut me up, and so I screamed louder, the terror rising inside me, overwhelming me.

After what seemed an eternity, Malcolm and Dad came running back up the side of the quarry, their arms full of bits of salvaged wood, wanting to know what I was screaming about. I couldn't possibly have told them the truth about how I'd been terrified by my own imagination and so, as I fought to speak through my tears and my sobs, I told them that a man had come out of the woods and threatened me. It almost didn't feel like lying because I was convinced there was a man out there who was after me.

Dad must have been convinced by my story because he told Malcolm to stay with me as he ran up the path looking for the man I'd described. Fortunately he didn't come across any lone men innocently out walking their dogs, or he might well have attacked them without stopping to ask any questions, and he returned a few minutes later to where Malcolm and I were waiting. We made our way back home with the salvaged wood.

The idea that this killer was after me had now taken a firm hold in my brain and I couldn't be alone at any time without the panic returning, making me run at full pelt to wherever I was meant to be going. Everyone became a suspect – neighbours, teachers, uncles or strangers – and I would scour their faces for any telltale signs of guilt, constantly certain that I had detected a furtive look or a word out of place.

With the tree gone from the front of the house, Dad had the brilliant idea of building a windmill out of lolly sticks over the stump. 'I'll pay you and your friends two pence for every twenty lolly sticks you bring to me,' he announced.

It was the best offer we'd ever had and so we set out in pairs to scour the streets for sticks so that we could claim our reward. I don't think the streets in that area have ever been so clean. We collected for weeks and when we couldn't find any more we started following ice-cream vans, watching for people buying lollies and following them until they discarded their sticks.

When we'd produced enough, Dad built the windmill and painted it white. For a couple of days I was so proud when people walked past and glanced into our garden. I felt we were posh. We were normal. I had the same feeling when one of Dad's workmates parked a car that they'd bought for scrap outside our house. I thought everyone would think we were the sort of family that owned a car. Then one night it rained and when we came out in the morning on the way to school we were greeted by the sight of the tree stump surrounded by a carpet of white sticks. I didn't think I would go back in and tell Dad; it would be better if he found out for himself. I was beginning to learn that he was easily upset if he was in a bad mood. I had discovered this as a result of talking too quickly when I was nervous, which was most of the time. Often my gabble became such a headlong rush that no one could understand a word of it, even though I knew exactly what I was talking about.

'I can't understand a fucking word you're saying,' Dad would shout at me as I fought to slow my thoughts, but the more nervous he made me, the faster I spoke.

The following year, 1977, was the Queen's Silver Jubilee and all the local people laid out long tables in a field behind Broadlea Street. Throughout the afternoon we ate and drank, wearing paper hats and sitting beneath balloons and bunting. Dad was the life and soul of the party, as always, and everyone was laughing, singing and joking. I loved being amongst the crowd, a normal child like all the others, running around between the tables and chairs, feeling safe and surrounded by good people, a part of everything that was going on. Grown-ups would ruffle my hair affectionately as I rushed past, as if I was a likeable young rascal and part of their community. I wanted so much to prolong that feeling of being safe and normal, because most of the time I didn't feel like this, and recent events had been making things worse.

In February of that year another woman's body had been found. Her name was Irene Richardson and the police were sure her killer was the same man who had killed Mum and Emily Jackson. The newspapers realised they now had a serial killer on their hands and they had a field day, drawing parallels with the infamous Victorian killer, Jack the Ripper. But he had killed prostitutes in the East End slums of London and it seemed to me as if they were saying that Mum and the other women were prostitutes too. Two months later there was another victim, Patricia Atkinson. All the previous victims' names were put back in the paper once more so that readers could relive the whole gruesome story from the start, and this time there was a picture of Mum as well. The photograph must have come from the police because it had been taken when she was eighteen and was arrested for shoplifting. It was a terrible picture, nothing like the twenty-eight-year-old woman I remembered. I was ashamed that other people who had never known her were seeing it and thinking that was what my mum was like. Other children at school who knew my surname were asking if Wilma McCann was my mum.

I was beginning to read the papers more, irresistibly drawn to them even though I didn't want to know what was in them, and learned that Mum had been stabbed fourteen times and hit over the head with a hammer. I couldn't believe that was possible. Nothing so terrible could have happened to my mum; they must have made a mistake. I forced myself to put the whole thing out of my mind, not to believe it. But two months later another girl, eighteen-year-old Jayne MacDonald, was killed on her way home and it looked like the work of the same man. I wasn't going to be allowed to escape from this story.

'I know who she is,' Sonia said when Jayne's picture appeared in the papers. 'She lived just a few doors up the street in Scott Hall Avenue. She used to babysit for us sometimes.'

Yet again the killer had struck close to our lives, as if showing me that he could get me, or any of us, any time he wanted. My mind was spinning. What was going on? Who was doing all these killings? Was anybody safe from this man? Why couldn't the police stop him?

Only two weeks after Jayne MacDonald's death, a man attempted to murder a girl called Maureen Long. When I heard the news I hated the fact that she had managed to escape when Mum hadn't. It seemed so unfair.

On Sonia's ninth birthday, 1 October 1977, the Ripper struck again, killing Jean Jordan in Manchester. Everywhere we went people were talking about it. They no longer bothered to lower their voices if we were around. The *Yorkshire Post* seemed to be able to find something to print about the story every day.

At the end of October the police announced that a £5 note had been found on one of the victims, which they claimed was a vital clue, and suggested they were close to nailing their man. They said on the evening news that they could trace the note back to the factories and places of work that it had been sent to and that it was only a matter of time before the truth was revealed. But nothing came of it.

Nothing ever seemed to come of any of their investigations. As far as I could see, the murderer was invincible, he could kill who he wanted, when he wanted and for as long as he wanted, because the police hadn't got a clue who he was or how to find him.

chapter four

murder in the house

Dad's job as a joiner meant that sometimes he was in work for several months at a time, hired by a sub-contractor on a building site somewhere, or he'd be unemployed for long stretches. Often he worked away from home and we didn't see him for days on end; at other times he would sit around the house or go down the pub.

It wasn't long before we realised just how much he liked to drink, but that was no surprise to us as we'd seen Mum after her nights out and most of the grown-ups we knew seemed to drink to some degree. But the booze always used to make Mum cheerful and funny, even if she was nursing a headache the next morning. It had a different effect on Dad, making him angry and bitter and violent. Once he was under the influence he would scream at Pauline and hit her with all his strength, just like he had hit Mum, like Keith had hit Mum. He had no control over his temper or his fists. We would huddle up in our beds, as we always had, listening to the battles raging throughout the house, every painful sound clear through the thin walls. Outside the house he was still everyone's best friend and the centre of attention at any gathering. In private he was turning into a monster.

The police kept issuing different photo-fit pictures of the man they said they were looking for in connection with all the murders and at one stage they said they were looking for a bearded Irishman.

I became terrified by all bearded men. From the kitchen, in the evening, looking out into the darkness of the back garden through our curtain-less windows, I expected the Ripper to appear from the shadows and reveal that he'd been watching the house all along. I hated being in the kitchen on my own and would shake uncontrollably if I had to be there without anyone else, running back to the safety of another room as quickly as possible.

As I lay in bed one night, listening to my father laying into Pauline downstairs, his aggressive Irish voice roaring up through the floor as he shouted endless torrents of abuse at her, I wondered if *he* might be the Yorkshire Ripper. It all came together in my overworked imagination. Hadn't he told me he hated Mum? Didn't he have an uncontrollable temper? Wasn't he perfectly happy to inflict pain on women and others who were weaker than him? Once when a young neighbour made the mistake of throwing a stone over our adjoining fence, which hit our kitchen window, Dad went to the cupboard where he kept his tools and took out a hammer. Storming out into the back garden, he managed to climb on top of the dustbin, despite his inebriated state, and swung the hammer through their kitchen window in a staggeringly vicious act of petty revenge. An hour later the police were knocking on our front door and Dad was arrested and taken down to the station. It didn't seem to me that there was much point in the police doing anything. To my impressionable young mind Dad seemed to be a law unto himself, a man so powerful that he could and would deal with any situation with violence and not worry about the consequences, just like the Ripper.

It made sense in the darkest moments of the night, when we were at his raging, drunken mercy. Not only did I suspect every other man in the world of being my potential assassin, I even began to wonder if the man who was supposed to be looking after me, protecting me, might be the one who wanted to murder me. There didn't seem to be any certainties, no security or refuge from the dangers of the world, even in my own home, my own bed.

On the second anniversary of Mum's burial, on 21 January 1978, the Ripper murdered his seventh victim, Yvonne Pearson, a twenty-one-year-old prostitute. Her body wasn't found until two months later, when the media went mad once more and another photo joined the tragic line-up of women's faces, including Mum's horrible teenage mug-shot, which was reprinted every time a new victim was added to the roll call. I never wanted to read the papers, but the billboards in the street would scream out their headlines with each new development and I would know that I wouldn't be able to avoid seeing Mum's face again.

Every day I tried to suppress all the fears and paranoid theories swilling about inside me. All around us people were becoming more and more suspicious. Everyone was terrified and everyone wondered if they knew the killer, were sleeping with him or related to him. Ten days later another young prostitute, eighteen-year-old Helen Rykta, joined the list. I knew what a prostitute was. I knew they stood on street corners and had sex with men for money. I don't remember anyone actually explaining it to me. I simply put together what I read in the papers with the evidence of my own eyes. I was willing to accept that this man did kill prostitutes, but if that was the case, why had Mum been his first victim? Out of all the women in Leeds, why had he chosen her?

So much was going on in my head, some of it imagined and some remembered, that when I recalled a long-haired man who had stayed with us when we lived with Mum I wondered if I should tell anyone about it. I confided in one of Gary Dudley's brothers. They must have talked about it amongst themselves because the next day I came home from school to find a police car parked outside the house. My heart was thumping as I came in and found Dad and Pauline sitting with a policeman in the living room.

'What did you mean when you said you remembered some-one living at your house?' the policeman asked.

'I can't remember much,' I confessed. 'I just know someone stopped there who wasn't Keith or my dad.'

I could tell by the look on Dad's face as the policeman asked me more questions that he wasn't happy about me dragging all this out again. I was dreading the policeman going but I couldn't think of anything to say that would make him stay longer.

As soon as he left, Dad exploded, as I'd thought he would, accusing me of lying and trying to draw attention to myself. He sent me to bed without any tea as punishment for bringing the police to his door. I didn't understand why he was so upset, because I was sure I wasn't lying. There definitely had been someone living at our house at some point. It wasn't till many years later that I discovered one of Mum's brothers came to live with us just after Dad left. Banished to my bedroom, I stood staring out at the white tower of the university and swore that if I thought of anything else in the future I would keep it to myself.

There were times when we got to do normal family things. Although she wasn't our real mum, and although she always took Dad's side against us in arguments, Pauline wasn't unkind to us herself, and sometimes she did nice things. When the mongrel dog that lived opposite us gave birth to a litter of pups, for instance, she decided we should have one of them. When we brought it home it was still a tiny bundle of white fluff.

'What are we going to call it?' I asked.

'Why don't we all think of a name,' Pauline suggested, 'write them down and put them in a hat?'

We did as she suggested and, when her choice was drawn out, the new member of our family was officially christened Winney. The name suited her and she grew to be a proper family pet, snuggling up to us when we were sitting watching television, although no one ever managed to house-train her, so she did leave little wet piles of dog mess for us to step in when we got up for school in the morning.

One Sunday afternoon Dad had been for his usual afternoon drink in the pub. We'd all had our dinner and he'd fallen asleep in his favourite chair when he was woken by the sound of Winney scratching on the front door to be let in. She'd come into season and a pack of local dogs had caught her scent and pursued her home. Furious at being disturbed, Dad stamped out to open the door and scooped Winney up, chasing the others away and bringing her into the house. He slammed the door behind him and I was pleased that he had wanted to protect Winney from the unwanted attentions of the pack outside. I expected Dad to bring her into the living room so I could make a fuss of her after her ordeal, but instead he carried her straight upstairs. I could hear him running the bath water and Winney was yelping, so I guessed he was going to give her a wash.

A few minutes later I heard Dad stomping back downstairs and expected Winney to come rushing in, shaking her wet coat all over the room, indignant and excited by the water, but there was no sign of her and Dad went straight out into the garden.

I didn't want to risk going outside and incurring his wrath; if he'd wanted me there he would have told me. So I went upstairs and peeked out of my bedroom window to see if I could work out what was going on. Dad was in the garden below, digging a hole and there was something lying on the ground beside him, covered in a sheet. Unable to believe the implications of this, I went into the bathroom. There was still some water in the tub, and it was stained pink with blood. He'd drowned Winney.

He finished his work in the garden and came back inside to his armchair. None of us dared to mention Winney's name in his presence.

By this time Dad was drinking heavily most nights, going to a local pub, the Sandford Arms, after work, before coming home to pick a fight with Pauline, which would often end up with him hitting her. She would regularly walk out on him and he would then go after her the next day and talk her into coming back. He obviously loved her and didn't want to lose her and he could be very persuasive when he was sober, each time promising to give up the booze for good. He would lay off for a while once she returned, but he'd soon lapse.

On Sunday nights the two of them would go out together. These evenings nearly always started with them leaving the house in high spirits and finished with him shouting abuse at her. One night he threw their Chinese takeaway over her head in his anger. Another night their row started in the bedroom.

'You wouldn't treat me like this if you were a real man,' we heard Pauline say.

Then there was a crash as he threw her to the floor, snarling, 'I'll show you a real man.'

She must have managed to get to her feet because we heard her running out of the bedroom, with him coming after her and following her into the bathroom, shouting abuse and hitting her just a few yards from where we were lying, petrified. It sounded as though he was going to kill her and the idea came back to me that he might be the Ripper. It was like having to listen to Mum being killed.

'*Daaaaaaaad!*' I shouted, stretching the one word out as far as I could.

The noises stopped. My scream had got through to his drunken brain and a few seconds later he lumbered into the bedroom. I could hear Pauline stumbling downstairs, throwing open the front door and escaping into the cold, dark, dangerous street in her nightgown.

'It's all right,' he muttered, 'everything's OK, your mum and me are just having a bit of an argument.'

Pauline was unable to walk upright because of the punctured lung he'd inflicted on her and had to crawl down the street on her hands and knees, gasping for breath, heading for

Auntie Katherine's house a mile and a half away. Dad didn't bother to go after her. He simply went to bed while we waited for our heartbeats to subside.

Pauline had to be hospitalised after that beating and when she got out she took Cheryl with her to her mother's. The house became dead without her and sweet, sensible Sonia stepped into her shoes, as she so often had. I decided that my dad was a bastard and I loathed him. Things seemed to be getting worse with time, not better. Why did Mum have to go and get murdered?

chapter five

the bully
reveals himself

The Ripper's ninth victim in May 1978 was another prostitute called Vera Millward. Now it seemed that all the women this man had killed, including Mum, would be for ever labelled as prostitutes in the minds of the newspaper-reading public, as if she had somehow deserved what had happened to her. Once, when I was at the house of a friend, a Ripper murder was reported on the news and my friend's mother made a contemptuous spitting noise as the faces of the Ripper's victims came up on the screen, including Mum's. 'They deserve everything they get,' she said.

Her words went through me like an electric shock. That was my mother she was talking about, as well as other normal, harmless women who had done nothing other than be in the wrong place at the wrong time. I sat very still, staring straight ahead, avoiding eye contact, unable to think what to say or how to react.

The articles in the *Yorkshire Post* contained more and more detail. They printed maps, pictures and poems that the victims had written. The paper had started a Ripper hotline, a reward was being offered and there were stories of women in the area taking karate lessons to protect themselves on the streets at night.

As I grew older I hated looking in mirrors. I hated my freckled face, my skinny little body and my ginger hair. I thought I was the ugliest and most worthless child I knew. My clothes were always bought from jumble sales and hung off me in all the wrong places. How could anyone ever want me when I was grown up? I wondered. But then it seemed pretty unlikely that I would live to be an adult anyway. The chances of the Ripper getting me on my own at some stage seemed very high. The fact that he had only killed women so far was irrelevant to me. He had chosen Mum at random, and all the other victims; why wouldn't he pick on me in just the same way? I wasn't even sure that it mattered that much if I was killed, but that didn't stop me from being very scared. I must have done something wrong to have been given such a bad life, I thought. Maybe I was being punished for being too cheeky to Mum when she was alive. We were certainly made to feel we were bad now, since Dad was always losing his temper and punishing one or other of us. We would seldom get through an evening meal without someone being sent up to bed for some petty offence. There never seemed to be any break from being worried or frightened or yelled at.

I'd started stealing chocolate bars or biscuits from other kids' school lunch-boxes. I despised myself for it but at the same time I longed for the taste of them so much and felt it was my right since we would never be given anything like that ourselves. I would make an excuse to go to the toilet when everyone else was in class and rifle quickly through the bags hanging in the cloakroom until I found something that took my fancy. I knew that if I was caught, Dad would beat me, and all my teachers and classmates would look down on me even more than they did already. My heart was constantly in my mouth while I committed the crimes, but I was lucky enough always to get away with it.

Angela was not so lucky. She and a school friend were caught helping themselves to sweets in the tuck shop and the teacher sent a note home with her. If that teacher had known what would happen I don't think she would have sent that letter.

Dad read it, silent and grim-faced, and sent her up to our bedroom. He then calmly found a piece of wood about a foot long and an inch-and-a-half thick, which he used to beat her from just above the back of her knees all the way up to the lower part of her back. The rest of us listened in horror, helpless as the blows rained down on her, unable to do anything to block out her screams or to stop Dad's furious attack. When he finally tired of hitting her, we could hear only Angela's sobs, but Dad didn't emerge from the room and we couldn't hear any voices. Sonia and I exchanged puzzled, frightened, silent looks.

Eventually he came downstairs, apparently satisfied that he had taught her a lesson. Sonia and I went in to see her as soon as he had gone out. Angela's face was puffy and streaked with tears as she told us that once he'd finished beating her he had lain down on the adjoining bed and just stared at her, saying nothing, taking long, slow drags on his cigarettes, savouring his power over her. A line of spent cigarette butts stood upright beside the bed, bearing witness to how long he had lain there, intimidating her. The back of Angela's legs and her back were literally black and blue. She was seven years old. I wanted to kill him.

My turn came when I stole some money from him. Dad never gave us any pocket money, having spent all his earnings on beer and gambling. All my friends seemed to have so much more than me and I felt that I should have just some of the things they took for granted. I'd spotted his jacket in the bedroom and crept in, my heart thumping, to see what I could find. The coins – 20p in all – clanked noisily in my sweaty palm as I lifted them out and I felt sure everyone downstairs had heard. I dashed back to the bedroom and hid them under the carpet, planning to go back for them later. By sheer bad luck, one of my sisters found the money when she was doing some sweeping and handed it over to Pauline, who had by then been persuaded by Dad to return to the house with Cheryl.

I was out playing in the street with some friends when Pauline called me into the living room and told me to sit on the sofa. She didn't say anything else, just sat silently in a chair as my stomach sank. Eventually she leaned down, lifted the corner of the imitation fur rug in front of us both and gently picked up the two 10p pieces, which were in the positions I had put them in, keeping her eyes on my face.

'I found them down the back of the toilet,' I lied. 'They must have fallen out of Dad's pocket.'

To my surprise she didn't send me straight to bed, but allowed me back out to play with my friends as if nothing had happened, but I didn't for a moment believe I was going to be allowed to get away with it and I dreaded Dad's return from work. My terror increased as the minutes ticked by. Finally he arrived and gave me a friendly wave from the gate. I waved back and tried to convince myself that Pauline wouldn't deliver me into his brutal hands. Then the door opened.

'Richard!' he shouted, and there was no doubting his anger. 'Get in the house, now.'

The other children looked at me. I felt I was walking to my execution as I returned to the house, every muscle trembling. He held a wooden stick.

'You're going to get one strike of the stick for every penny you've stolen,' he told me.

Even though I knew there was no point, I screamed that I hadn't stolen the money as the blows fell on my naked behind. My friends were standing outside the house, silently listening to my agonised cries. When he'd finished beating me he sent me to bed. I wished I were dead.

I started having dreams about murdering him, and I never felt any remorse after completing the act. There were times when he had sent me upstairs for some trivial misdemeanour like knocking his chair with the door while he was dozing, and I would sit in my room, staring at the white university tower outside the window and wishing I could be with Mum, wherever she might be now. What was the point of going on living when you never received any love, just one punishment after another? Sonia, Donna, Angela and I felt like second-class citizens, always made to go to bed by seven o'clock in the evening, while Cheryl was allowed to stay up watching television as late as she liked. It was as if we were an inconvenience from Dad's previous life. Sometimes, when I had been banished to the freezing bedroom, I would lie down on the bed and hold my breath, hoping that I would be able to suffocate myself. Each time I failed to die I would try again until eventually I would fall asleep. There was a railway line running close to the house and I fantasised about lying down on the tracks just as one of the new Intercity 125 trains was approaching, placing myself so that my head would be cut cleanly off. I imagined this would guarantee a quick and painless death. I also dreamed of throwing myself off one of the many blocks of high-rise flats in the area, so that I would never have to feel anything ever again. But I was too much of a coward to go through with it.

School provided some respite. I felt safe amongst the crowds of children, watched over by teachers and other staff, and at times I felt almost normal. I found myself starting to look forward to playtime and a game I'd started to play with the girls in my class. It was a kind of tag and most of the time it was them chasing me, but it had more meaning to me than a simple game of chase. When they caught me I experienced the most intense feelings of pleasure, not of a sexual kind, but just the comfort of contact with a female, a closeness that I must have been missing at home, apart from with Sonia. I just wanted to be close to them and to be touched.

The Yorkshire Ripper, whoever he was, seemed to be enjoying his notoriety now. He began writing letters to the police, taunting them, telling them they would never catch him. When he struck his tenth victim, Josephine Whitaker, in April 1979, it was after eleven months of inactivity, long enough for us all to wonder if he had given up and would now never be caught, but not long enough for us to forget that he was still out there and that he might strike again at any moment. A few months later the police received tapes of a Geordie man's voice claiming to be the Ripper.

'My name's Jack,' he said. 'You are no nearer to catching me than you were four years ago.'

He meant the night he killed Mum. When I heard the voice on the news I was actually listening to the bastard who had taken Mum away from me. How could the whole police force be so helpless to stop him? The media kept playing and playing the message, hoping that someone would recognise the voice, and every time it came on I had to leave the room, my stomach churning.

One weekend we were visiting Uncle Isaac and Auntie Vicky and we went down to the local Liberal Club on the Sunday afternoon so they could drink beer, socialise, play bingo or listen to a band while we sat quietly drinking Coke and eating crisps. Then from nowhere the Ripper's voice came out over the tannoy system, filling every corner of the room, leaving us no way of escaping. We froze, expecting the adults to whisk us out of the room, but no one seemed to connect us with the message, or seemed at all concerned that we were there, listening to our mother's murderer boasting about his crimes. If the adults didn't think it was unreasonable, I thought, then it must be me who was wrong. But at least now that I had heard the Ripper's voice, I knew that Dad wasn't the killer.

The more the Ripper teased the police, the more frenzied the media became. New clues, descriptions and headlines came out every day, with thousands of calls coming in to the Ripper hotline. In September, just before we were due to go back to school, he killed a Bradford student called Barbara Leach, having promised that he would find another victim that month.

But I was learning how to deal with the whole Ripper business. I tried to ignore any public mention of it that I came across, keeping my memory of Mum separate. I'd discovered that if I thought of Mum in the context of the murders, the pictures that came into my head were too painful to bear. I'd erected barriers and put certain memories into boxes in order to cope. It didn't always work in keeping the images at bay, but it was effective enough for me to be able to function most of the time. I just wanted to be a normal child.

In 1980, when I was ten, I got a job delivering papers for the local newsagent. On 21 August I remember clearly the front-page headline: 'RIPPER FEAR AFTER NAKED BODY FOUND'. Every time I took a paper, folded it and posted it through a letterbox, the words screamed out at me. I went as fast as I could, desperate to be rid of the papers. The victim this time was Marguerite Walls, an office worker who had been attacked as she made her way home from working late. There was no suggestion that she was a prostitute. It seemed this man hated all women.

I, on the other hand, was starting to hate all men. I knew the feeling was irrational but I couldn't stop it from growing inside my head. I would listen to every man I passed in the street, trying to spot the Geordie accent that had taunted me over the airwaves. I was convinced the Ripper must live in the Leeds area, even if some of the killings had happened further afield.

When I got home from my paper round that day in August, I went straight up to the bedroom and lay down on the bed, my head spinning as I started to plot my revenge on the world. I wanted people to suffer for what I was having to go through.

I decided I would travel around the region, killing as many men as possible. I intended to identify lone males, run up behind them and hit them over the head with a hammer. I would strike in different areas of Yorkshire, making it seem random, and imagined a large map of the area on the walls of a police station with pins marking each of the spots where I had struck. Eventually the pins would be joined together, like a dot-to-dot puzzle, by some bright detective and they would see a sign like the letter 'R', which would stand both for 'Richard' and for 'Ripper'. I would settle the score for all the pain I'd been put through by whatever force it was in society that was plotting to make me so unhappy. I had been surrounded with talk of murder and bloodshed and pain, so it seemed fitting that I should become an active part of it. I would become somebody important if I carried out a campaign of mass murder, and being caught grew to be part of the fantasy. Anything would be better than being a worthless nobody who was never allowed to feel good about himself. Since there were no signs anywhere in the adult world of the love that I craved so much, what had I got to lose?

Dad's reign of terror was growing worse at home. Early one Saturday evening I walked into the house and heard shouting. It was not an unusual occurrence but it still made my heart sink. Dad was in a fury because someone had helped themselves to half a Bounty chocolate bar that he had left in the bedroom. For a moment it was a relief to discover that the argument was about something that had nothing to do with me, but then I realised no one else was planning to own up, which meant that we were all going to be in the frame for the crime.

Dad pushed the sofa back against the wall to clear a space on the living-room floor. 'Get down,' he ordered us, 'all four of you, on your hands and knees. Get into the press-up position.'

We did as he told us. Cheryl didn't have to do it because, Dad reasoned, she always got given her own sweets and chocolates and wouldn't have any need to steal. This didn't seem such a bad punishment, but none of us had ever tried to hold a position like that before. The pain in our arms built very quickly to an agonising level.

'Come on, which of you has taken it?' he shouted.

We each denied the charge vehemently, although the pain was becoming almost intolerable and I wondered if perhaps Cheryl had taken the chocolate after all and was enjoying watching us all suffer. After five minutes Angela and Donna started to cry.

'If your arms give way I'm going to be kicking you back up again,' he promised.

'It was me,' Sonia said, as her arms buckled and she fell to the floor.

'So, you would put your brother and sisters through all this for a piece of chocolate, would you, you lying little cow?' he yelled as we all lay collapsed on the floor . 'You're nothing but a little thief.'

'It wasn't me,' Sonia said angrily, 'but I'll take the punishment!'

'No,' he bawled. 'I want to know who would let someone else take their punishment because they won't own up to something.'

'It was me,' Angela shouted before he could force us back into the agonising position. 'I took it.' She burst into tears again, knowing that she would be in for a beating.

'I'm not going to hit you this time,' he said, to all our surprise, 'but I suggest your brother and sisters remember what you were willing to put them through here. You're the black sheep of this family and I want everyone to remember that.'

I'm ashamed to say that his tactics were partly successful because I never did see Angela in quite the same light again. From then on she seemed to be picked on for even the slightest thing and I felt very sorry for her. When all of us were there for a meal there were never quite enough chairs for everyone to sit around the table, so Angela would be the one who would have to eat her dinner standing up at the kitchen surface. She was nearly always the one who was made to wash up all the dishes afterwards.

Although we were given a meal in the evening, there wasn't always very much and we would often still feel hungry afterwards. One night, as Angela was washing the dishes on her own in the kitchen, she spotted a piece of chicken that Dad had left on his plate. Glancing furtively over her shoulder she popped it into her mouth and bit a piece off. As she was chewing it, Dad suddenly rushed into the kitchen. Panic-stricken, she shoved her hand into the washing-up water to try to hide the rest of the meat and attempted to swallow her mouthful before he noticed, but she wasn't quick enough.

'What are you eating?' he demanded.

'Nothing,' she mumbled.

'Show me what you've got in your hand.'

Reluctantly she lifted her hand out of the water, with the dripping chicken still between her fingers.

'You animal!' Dad sneered, concluding that she'd been eating food from the dirty water.

Angela must have felt even more worthless and unloved than the rest of us during those years. She didn't seem to be able to do or say anything to stop him from bullying her. We could do nothing to help her, being too anxious not to bring the spotlight of his temper back to us, and so she just had to cope with the persecution on her own.

Dad always told me that whatever punishment he was doling out to us was nothing compared to how his father had treated him as a boy. 'He used to make me stand in a corner in the living room in darkness for whole nights,' he explained once. 'He would come down to check on me every so often and if he found me asleep on the floor he would kick me awake.'

Years later Sonia asked one of Dad's sisters why he was like he was.

'He was the youngest in the family,' our aunt replied, 'and the most spoilt. He never got hit.'

In November a sixteen-year-old student called Jacqueline Hill from Middlesborough was murdered in Leeds, the Ripper's thirteenth victim. After five years of it I now found that I was able to read the accounts of this poor girl's death in the papers without feeling it was anything to do with me. I had finally managed to find a way of blocking it out.

Christmas arrived, with all the usual reminders that Mum wasn't with us and never would be again, and then in the New Year the police announced that a man was 'helping them with their enquiries'.

chapter six
sutcliffe is caught

It was the arrest of the century. Everyone was talking about it in January 1981, but no one felt able to explain to us what was happening. What did 'helping the police with their enquiries' mean? Gradually, by listening to snippets of conversation and news bulletins, I began to put together a picture of what had happened. The man who had murdered my mother had been caught.

The subject was still not mentioned inside the house. It didn't seem to occur to Dad, or any other adults, that we might have feelings or fears about the capture of this man. We were left to think it through for ourselves.

On the news the chief constable of Yorkshire, Ronald Gregory, was pictured with his team, beaming and saying that he was 'absolutely delighted'. His words made me feel sick. The phrase stayed in my head in the same way the Ripper's tapes had. *I* wasn't 'absolutely delighted'.

But at least the whole business was over at last and now I wanted it to be forgotten as quickly as possible. I was soon to find out there was no hope of that happening.

The media had been running the same stories over and over again during the previous five years. Now they had a whole new cache of information. The monster had actually been caught and the public wanted to know every detail about how the police had done it and who the man was. We discovered that his name was Peter Sutcliffe, that his wife was called Sonia and the couple had been on the verge of adopting a child. He was a Bradford man, with no Geordie accent, and we heard an endless stream of stories from his neighbours and work colleagues as they all cashed in on their proximity to infamy. We saw photographs of wedding certificates and heard remand details; nothing about him was too trivial to be paraded out into the public gaze.

It seemed the media had gauged the public's level of interest exactly right because crowds of people turned up in the street where the Sutcliffes lived; so great was the crush that their neighbours asked to have the area cordoned off. I couldn't understand why people who had no connection with the man or his deeds could be so fascinated. I didn't like the idea that he was being given so much importance; he didn't deserve to be a celebrity. Nevertheless, he seemed to be on everybody's lips. Dad even came home from the pub one afternoon with a Ripper joke.

The papers were competing for the stories of all the women who'd been attacked by Sutcliffe but had managed to survive. Every week another one appeared under huge, garish headlines.

In May 1981 Peter Sutcliffe was finally charged with the murder of thirteen women and the attempted murder of seven others.

The trial passed – every one of us pretending we didn't care, that we weren't disturbed by each new revelation – and Sutcliffe was found guilty. The Ripper I had been so afraid of was locked away and the streets were safe again.

Now I should have been free to get on with the business of growing up. I was developing a sharp interest in the world around me, devouring facts from encyclopaedias and atlases, looking up different countries and imagining how I might be able to start a new life somewhere else, far away from the hurtful memories that would come back at unexpected moments every day. I loved the idea of escaping from my past and starting somewhere new where no one had heard of Peter Sutcliffe or of my mother's death.

By now I was in the second year at middle school, with Sonia in the year above me. People were always asking if she was my sister, making me feel very proud. Donna was in the year below me and sometimes she would bring someone to me and ask me to confirm that I was her big brother. Maybe she felt as proud of me as I was of Sonia. I hope so. Other kids would sometimes come up to us now and ask if it was true that the Ripper had killed our mum. A boy who was known as 'the Cock of the School' said that if ever anyone gave me any trouble to let him know and he would sort them out.

We were still having to wear clothes Pauline had managed to find at jumble sales and I always dreaded the day when someone would spot me wearing an old item they'd thrown out. Trying to get by on the money that Dad brought home must have been a constant struggle, especially with so many of us to care for, and Pauline did her best. She would buy shoes with the thickest soles possible so that they would last. They were ugly things and my teacher obviously felt sorry for me because she asked what size I wore and told me she had an old pair of shoes at home I could have if I wanted. Although it was kind of her, it made me feel deeply ashamed.

Over the next year or so the Ripper story kept resurfacing in the papers as various surviving victims applied for damages against Peter Sutcliffe for the injuries they'd suffered at his hands. Whenever I read that one of them had been awarded thousands of pounds I felt angry at the thought that they had survived and Mum hadn't, and that they got compensated while we didn't even have enough money for new clothes.

When Pauline and Dad went out together on Sunday nights, Sonia and I would take it in turns to babysit the others. Together we would go through all the food cupboards and the fridge in search of anything edible that would stave off the constant hunger pains, even if it was just a raw sausage, a couple of biscuits or an Oxo cube. If we found anything we felt it was our treat and didn't share it with Donna and Angela. I guess we weren't malnourished, but we did feel hungry most of the time.

One Sunday night we heard Dad and Pauline come in early. Pauline was crying. At the time Sonia and I were sharing the smallest room and had single beds with a gap down the middle just wide enough to squeeze through. We both lay under the blankets, hardly daring to breathe as we waited to see what would happen next. We heard Dad shouting abuse at Pauline and when his heavy footsteps started up the stairs we both closed our eyes and pretended to be asleep. I was certain Dad would know I'd sneaked downstairs to watch television while they were out and was coming to punish me. The room was completely dark, with only a sliver of light spilling in through a gap in the door from the hallway outside. Even with my eyes shut I could sense the light growing brighter and knew that Dad had opened the door. He was shouting his usual abuse, but was too drunk to make any sense. I kept my eyes tight shut. Suddenly I was aware of him pushing between the beds and felt his hand covering my face, squeezing my jaws with his strong fingers as if trying to crush them, his palm covering my mouth so that I could only breathe through my nose. I forced myself to lie still, fighting back the panic and the urge to struggle, desperate not to anger him any further. I could sense that his other hand was doing the same to Sonia's face. Then he bent close and I could smell the booze on his breath as he put his mouth over my nose and closed his teeth. He was bloody biting me! It felt like being attacked by a wild animal and I just lay there, wishing he would drop dead. He couldn't have bitten with all his strength because the pain was not great, but the fear and disgust were overwhelming. Then, just as suddenly as he'd started, he stopped. He then did the same to Sonia before straightening up and shuffling out of the room to bed.

I thought nothing he could do to us would surprise me now, but I was soon proved wrong.

Around Broadlea Street there was a mixture of boys and girls who used to go around together and one sunny Sunday afternoon we were all playing British bulldogs in the field behind the houses. The game changed, as so often happens with children of that age, to a game of kiss-catch. The girls would run around and we would catch them, one at a time, and claim our kisses. The excitement was building and one boy started showing off, pulling down the knickers of one of the younger girls who was wearing a skirt. We all thought it was hysterically funny, apart from the girl herself, of course. The game finished and we all went about our business without giving the incident a second thought.

Eventually, as the evening drew in, I was called in to have my weekly Sunday night bath. Now that Sonia and I were older we were no longer expected to bath together, which was a relief as it had been starting to become a little embarrassing, but I still tended not to get much privacy in the bathroom as Dad always seemed to choose that moment to come in for a pee.

As I lay in the bath I heard a knock on the kitchen door, which was directly beneath the bathroom. I could hear muffled voices coming up through the floor but couldn't make out the words. Someone was talking to Dad and it didn't sound as if they were very happy. A few minutes later I heard the back door close and Dad's footsteps ascended the stairs. I assumed he was coming to use the toilet.

When he walked into the room, however, he lowered the toilet lid and sat down on it very calmly, just looking at me. He was making me feel deeply uneasy and I knew he was doing it on purpose. He always enjoyed playing cat and mouse with people.

'Have you had a good day, Richard?' he asked smugly, and I knew he was laying a trap for me.

'How do you mean?' I asked, wishing I wasn't naked and in the bathtub, but unable to get out while he was sitting there. I discreetly tried to cover myself. I knew he'd been drinking, which meant he was dangerous and unpredictable. He placed the cigarette he was smoking carefully on the window sill and I knew something was about to happen but had no idea what.

With a sudden explosion of movement he jumped off the toilet, grabbed my neck with both his powerful hands and pushed me under the water. My arms and legs thrashed wildly and ineffectually in the air as he held me under. I could hear him shouting but I couldn't make out what he was saying. All I could see was the froth of white bubbles as I thrashed around, fighting for breath, panic-stricken and remembering how easily he had disposed of Winney.

'No, Dad, no,' I pleaded as I came to the surface for a few seconds before he plunged me back below the water again. I had no way of escaping. The only way out of the bath was upwards and he was there and twenty times stronger than me. I was completely at his mercy and I thought he intended to kill me.

Then he stopped and sat down on the toilet again as if nothing had happened. He told me the father of the little girl whose knickers had been pulled down in the field had been round to complain.

'If I ever hear of you doing anything like that ever again,' he said, 'I'll bloody drown you.' Then he picked up his cigarette calmly, and walked out of the room.

In May 1982 I read that Sutcliffe was appealing against his conviction on the grounds of diminished responsibility. I didn't understand what it meant but I didn't like the idea that he might be let off. It felt as if he was continuing to taunt us, even from inside prison, and I was glad when the court denied his appeal.

The strain of being the sensible one for so many years appeared to be becoming too much for Sonia. She and her friends started buying glue, putting it into a bag and breathing in the fumes. Sonia knew that what she was doing would make Dad angry and said she did it partly as revenge. I remembered a time some years back when Sonia and a friend, Louise, used to nick cigarette ends from the ashtrays and go into the playing fields to smoke them. One afternoon Mum came back early and caught them, ordering them back into the kitchen. It was obvious from her face she'd had a drink or two, which meant she was in a good mood. She asked them how often they did it.

'Only on Saturdays,' Sonia confessed. Mum howled with laughter, gave them a couple of the bananas that she always bought in town and sent them out to play again. Sonia's friend was shocked to be let off so lightly, imagining Sonia would be in for a hiding. She couldn't believe it when Sonia said Mum never hit us.

Like me it seemed as if Sonia was carrying the weight of Mum's memory in private. Unlike me, however, she'd always tried to take responsibility for all of us and be a replacement mother.

None of us was ever allowed to forget the shadow that hung over our past. Peter Sutcliffe's bearded face continued appearing in the papers as one spurious story after another kept the saga going, feeding the public's endless appetite for details. At the end of each school day Sonia and I would meet and we just had to exchange looks to know that we had both seen his picture in the papers again.

It wasn't just Sonia and me who were suffering. Donna was finding her schoolwork difficult and her report said that she needed extra help with her maths. Dad decided that he would take on the job of drumming it into her head. One night, after we'd eaten, he tried to tell her the way to do a certain sum, but she just wasn't getting it. The rest of us went up to bed, leaving them to it in the kitchen. I lay with my ear to the floor, listening to them downstairs, hoping his anger wouldn't get out of control. He was yelling at her every time she got it wrong and I knew he was hitting her because I could hear crying and yelps of pain. The more he shouted abuse at her, the harder she was finding it to think straight. I wanted to run downstairs and kill him, but I was too scared. To me he still seemed the most powerful man in the world. But we couldn't sleep while our little sister was being so badly treated and Sonia and I just looked at each other, our teeth clenched and tears in our eyes.

On another evening he kicked and punched Angela so viciously in her bedroom that she brought up the meat and potatoes she'd just eaten for dinner all over her bedclothes.

By the time Sonia was fourteen, she was staying out later and later, defying Dad but still scared enough of him that she would try to be home before he returned from the pub, swaggering and swaying up the path, looking for a fight.

I often decided that the best plan was to go out. I liked going to other people's houses and seeing how normal families lived, families where the fathers weren't always angry and where not every penny was spent in the pub. I knew I shouldn't hang around my friends' houses when they were eating their family meals, but I did, waiting in the gardens until they were finished, feeling very jealous. Sometimes their parents would tactfully suggest that it was time I went home for my dinner and I would mutter something inaudible by way of an excuse.

There were moments when I would get tantalising glimpses of what life could have been like if Dad had been able to control his temper and his drinking. He once came to watch me playing in the local rugby team on a Sunday morning. There was a boy on the opposing team who looked about two years older than the rest of us, a giant of a boy. At one point in the game, he'd got past everyone else and was striding towards the touchline with me as the only hope left for our side. I ran behind him, closing the gap until I was just an arm's length away. My only hope was a flying tackle, something I'd never attempted before, but I was determined to impress Dad. With one final leap I dived onto his legs and brought him down just yards from scoring. I had no idea I was capable of such a feat and I was glowing with pride as I pulled myself back to my feet, thrilled that Dad had been there to see it. He never mentioned it.

Things between Sonia and Dad were getting worse and worse, and when Sonia pinched some money from a jar that Pauline used to save coins I knew she was going to receive a good beating. Dad had been drinking, as usual, and it was late on a Friday afternoon when he got home. We were all in the living room when Pauline told him what had happened. Dad dragged Sonia out into the hall by her clothes, slamming the door behind him. Sonia was screaming and I heard her fall onto the bottom of the stairs, Dad landing punches on her like a boxer. I pleaded with Pauline to stop him.

She hesitated then opened the door. 'Gerry,' she shouted, 'that's enough now.'

He came back into the living room, panting as if he had just sprinted the 100 metres.

I couldn't bring myself to look at him. I ran out of the house while Sonia was sent up to bed. It was late summer and still light outside, but inside the house it was as if a new and more terrible demon had been released.

Sonia wasn't allowed to get out of bed all weekend, and even had to eat her meals there. By Monday morning she was still in too much pain to be able to walk to school without other people seeing there was something terribly wrong. All week she had to stay in her room, night and day. Dad had calmed down but he refused to say her name, referring to her as 'she'.

After a week, when Dad wasn't there, we received a visitor. The smartly dressed man, who arrived in a gleaming new red car, explained that he was from the child protection unit of the Social Services and he'd been asked to visit the house after an anonymous call from a member of the public. Pauline looked very ill at ease and Sonia agreed to go to the hospital for a check-up.

Everyone was very caring and sympathetic at the hospital, reminding her of how kind people had been to us just after Mum had died. An X-ray showed that her shoulder had been badly damaged. It was no wonder that she had been in pain. She was admitted and kept for two days under observation. The doctors logged every bruise on her body and estimated how old each one might be from the colour. The fresh ones were different shades of purple and black, while older ones were fading and turning yellow.

'Do you want to go back home?' a doctor asked after two days.

'No way,' she replied. She felt sad at the thought of being separated from the rest of us, but couldn't bear to face Dad now that the authorities had been called in. She knew how badly he would react.

The Social Services tried to find Sonia a place in a local care home, but they were all full. The only space they could find was at Westwood Grange, a lock-up for disruptive children, which was more like a prison than a home and some way from our house, but was still preferable to being at Dad's mercy. For the six weeks she was at Westwood she was able to feel normal because all the other kids came from families like ours, or even worse. Some of the other kids had been involved with prostitution; some were arsonists, bullies and shoplifters. The boys there all fancied her, which made her feel that she wasn't as worthless as Dad always said she was. After six weeks the authorities managed to find her a place in a council home, which was more like Beckett's Park, in a nicer area of Leeds. She moved to Benjamin Gott High School, which was nearer to our house so we were able to meet her sometimes after school.

The house seemed very different without her there and no one told the rest of us exactly where she'd gone or whether we would see her again. Once again, when there was something serious going on in the family, we received no explanation. Dad just told us that Sonia was a bad person who'd brought trouble to the house. But Christmas that year wasn't the same without her.

chapter seven

sniffing

I began to feel that my relationship with Sonia, which had been the strongest of my life since Mum had gone, was slipping through my fingers.

But when I began to attend the same high school, Benjamin Gott, I saw her every day and I enjoyed myself there. One of Sonia's teachers made a big fuss of me and I guessed that she must know about what was going on in our house. I liked playing the clown in class, constantly trying to think of witty comments to say to the teachers, believing that the other kids would like me more if I made them laugh. I wasn't quite so confident when it came to chatting up the girls, but none of the other guys in the gang I formed had girlfriends either, so I didn't feel too bad.

The gang all lived within a mile or so of one another. Steven had been a friend since primary school and lived in the next street. He was good-looking and wore all the latest fashions, which meant the girls fancied him. Danny lived round the corner, but had attended a different middle school. His parents had split up but he seemed to be happy at home. Charlie had also been around since primary school. Once he pinched his mother's family allowance book and we spent all the money that was meant for her shopping. The police were called and we all got into serious trouble. Arnie was the other one in the gang who came from a broken home, but at least his mum, who was often drinking in the house, seemed to understand that lads would be lads.

We started sniffing glue in just the same way Sonia had. It was a buzz and made us feel different. We laughed a lot and thought we were really funny. It provided, I suppose, some escape from the less attractive realities of our lives. We did it in different places and it bonded us together. After a few weeks, however, the others grew tired of the game and stopped doing it, realising that it made them feel bad as much as it made them feel good, and that it was bound to get them into trouble sooner or later. Maybe they were able to see themselves more clearly than I could, and didn't like the look of what they saw, but for some reason I didn't want to give up. Each afternoon, when I got home from school, I would go to my room, spray deodorant into a bag and inhale it, losing myself in my own little world for hours. With the fumes numbing my brain, I no longer felt the need to go out with my mates after school and they started to notice that I was staying in, which puzzled them since they knew that our house wasn't a great place to be.

Part of me wanted to break the habit, but I just couldn't resist the sensation. So I was glad when my friends realised what I was doing and made it clear that if I didn't stop they were going to have nothing more to do with me. I wasn't so far gone that I didn't know that I needed them more than I needed the aerosols and I made myself stop. I will always be grateful to them for that and was pleased that when I really put my mind to something, I was able to do it. I so nearly became an addict, just as so many people in my family became addicted to drink, but I was able to pull myself away from the self-destructive behaviour when I had an incentive to do so.

I put as much effort into my schoolwork as I could and managed to stay in the top stream. I was proud of that and knew it would keep Dad off my back because he was always keen I should do well. Now Sonia was gone from the house and I was getting older he seemed to be mellowing towards me a little. In fact I felt so confident of our relationship that I actually decided to play a little practical joke on him. Using a typewriter in our classroom I wrote him a letter, supposedly from the headmaster, explaining that due to my high IQ I'd been chosen to represent the school on a television programme called *Blockbusters*, and sent it through the post. Dad was delighted and told all his friends down the pub. I kept it going for a couple of weeks, then told him the truth. Amazingly he saw the funny side of it. It seemed that our relationship might be improving at last.

During the summer holidays Pauline announced that she was pregnant again and all I could think was that the poor baby was going to have to spend its childhood with Dad. I couldn't understand how Pauline could let that happen to her own children.

When I heard that one of Peter Sutcliffe's fellow inmates had tried to smash the Ripper's face with a broken glass jar I felt very happy that someone who didn't even know me was willing to do that on my behalf. Everyone else hated him as much as I did. But I couldn't understand why his attacker was going to have to face charges. Wasn't it just what everyone should want to do to a monster who had ruined so many other people's lives? When I saw a picture of the scar on Sutcliffe's face I was disappointed that it didn't seem to be very big.

The attacker was found guilty of the assault and given a further five years in prison.

At school I decided to put myself forward for a public speaking competition. I'd never done anything like it before, so I decided to talk about something that was dear to my heart. A few years earlier Dad had built a pigeon loft and had started to keep birds, as well as the greyhound he already had. He'd got the idea from a guy who used to walk past the house with a basket of birds and sometimes stopped to chat about his hobby. Whenever Dad was away I had to look after them for him. It wasn't that I was particularly fond of them, but I'd enjoyed having the responsibility and I was very confident about handling them. I used to feed and water them, and take the young birds ten miles away to the bus terminus in their basket to give them their first taste of flying home. Mostly it was a chore, slipping about in the mud in the morning, but there were perks, like when Dad gave me £2 to buy them food and I spent £1.50, keeping the change for myself. I was sure I could talk on the subject for ten minutes without too much trouble.

Writing the speech came quite naturally to me, although I had to ask Dad about one or two things, which he was very pleased to tell me, happy to teach his son something new. I was determined not to make a fool of myself and once the speech was written I went over and over it for hours on end so that I wouldn't have to work from a script on stage. I was sure it would look much better if it seemed I was talking without notes. Even though I knew it backwards, forwards and upside-down, I was still incredibly nervous on the day of the competition, my stomach spinning all the way to school. As we filed into the hall I felt physically sick with nerves and wished I'd never started on such a dumb scheme. How could I stand up in front of the whole school, and who was going to be interested in pigeons anyway? But it was too late to go back now. I was committed.

I was the last one on and I listened to the others as they talked about history and tanks. They had lots of posters pinned up on boards and read from notes in front of them.

Then it came to my turn and I walked up on stage, feeling numb with fear. Before me stretched a sea of upturned faces, all waiting to hear what I had to say. Knowing what I was talking about gave me enough confidence to get started and I thought that the faces were looking slightly interested. They certainly weren't laughing or booing me off the stage. I hadn't got any posters to pin up, but as a finale I did have a live pigeon waiting at the side of the stage in a travelling basket. As I got near to the end I walked over and lifted the bird out of the basket, handling it as easily as if it were a puppy. I extended its wing to show the colour of the feathers and then carried it off-stage to the emergency exit at the side of the hall, opened the door and threw it up into the sky, so that everyone could see it flying away in the direction of my house. I answered a few questions from the audience and then it was all over. I stood there as they applauded loudly, feeling that I was going to burst with pride. I was actually being noticed and appreciated. I'd done something good that people liked. I wasn't worthless after all.

The next morning the results of the competition were announced, in reverse order and when my name was read out as the winner it was all I could do to stop myself from dissolving into tears. I was walking on air for days afterwards, especially when all the teachers congratulated me whenever they passed me in the corridors.

* * *

The stories about the Ripper kept appearing. There were articles about the police investigation that led to the arrest, and about relatives of Sutcliffe's who had to be moved because of attacks, and about more victims wanting compensation. Policemen were releasing their memoirs of the case and everyone seemed to have something to say, but there was never any mention of us and what we'd been through. It was as if it had never happened to us, as if we weren't owed any sort of compensation for losing our mum, as if Sutcliffe was someone important and our mum wasn't.

'When you're eighteen,' Auntie Vicky told us, 'you'll be able to claim some sort of criminal compensation.' But Dad never said anything and we would never have dared bring up the subject. Later I went to see a solicitor myself and asked him if he thought we would be due anything. He told me he would look into it but he needed a copy of the death certificate. I went to the records office in Leeds and was given a copy. It said 'MURDER' in large letters and gave details of exactly how Mum had died. I walked out of the offices in a daze and wandered around the city centre trying to gather my thoughts before going home. Although I had always known that she had been killed, it was different seeing it confirmed in a document that was simultaneously so official and so personal, as opposed to the dramatised accounts I had read in the newspapers. What had happened was a matter of record and could never be removed; it was an indelible fact and no matter how long I lived or what I did, I could never change that. In the end we were told we weren't due any compensation because Mum hadn't been working and so there was no loss of earnings.

In April 1986 Pauline gave birth to a boy called Daniel. He looked like Dad and I couldn't help but feel sorry for the life he was likely to have to endure. On the first Saturday afternoon after getting back from hospital, when Pauline heard that Sonia was visiting one of her friends up the road, she sent Angela up to ask her to come and see Daniel while Dad was out at the pub. Sonia came round and held Daniel in her arms and Pauline chatted to her as if she was interested in what she was up to. It seemed she was sorry for everything that had happened in the past and wished things had been different. Sonia didn't stay long because she knew Dad would hit the roof if he came back and found her there unexpectedly.

The following month a book about the Yorkshire Ripper called *Somebody's Husband, Somebody's Son* was published, which put the story in the papers again. Sutcliffe's face stared out at me from beneath the headlines once more.

I'd got myself a job delivering for the local milkman, who paid £10 each week. He would pick me up at four-thirty in the morning, which was hard, but it was worth it just to have some money of my own. At last I could buy some of the things other people had, going into Leeds city centre on the bus to shop for clothes or records or whatever took my fancy.

Whereas I had once been so good at distancing myself from the Ripper's crimes, I now found that I was drawn into bookshops where I would go to the crime sections and look for books about murders, looking up 'Sutcliffe' and 'Ripper' in the indexes and turning to the pages that contained information about him. I would then stand in the shop, reading, half wanting everyone who passed by to know that it was my mum I was reading about, that I was linked to this monster and that it was causing me enormous pain which I couldn't express. As long as I was reading about her, I felt I was still back there with Mum in a time when I was her favourite and her best boy, the one who made her laugh and who was always getting sent to bed for being cheeky. I wished I was back on her lap in the hospital waiting room, snuggled up, safe and secure and loved. I wanted to understand more of what had happened that evening, why she had decided to get into the car with that man, how they had met. All I discovered was that she had been seen having a drink in a club called the Room at the Top and eating chips by the side of the road, thumbing a lift. Sutcliffe must have stopped to give her a lift and it would certainly have been in character for her to have been that trusting of a complete stranger. It's also possible they had met at the club earlier as well.

Another part of me watched what I was doing in those shops and told me that I shouldn't be there, that it wasn't normal to be so obsessed by a murderer. But what was normal about our lives? I'd never been taught how to handle what had happened to me, how to rationalise all the things that were going on in my mind. I felt that I was a fraud, that I was just acting the same as other people. It was hard work keeping up an act like that all the time.

As I grew older, my friends and I were allowed to wander further from our homes on our own and we started visiting the local canal and swimming in the locks. It was exciting and dangerous and we loved it. We would fill a lock up to the brim and then jump in. Every now and again someone would open the sluice gates, which would send the water thrashing into the lock from the one above, pushing us against the far side with the force of the currents. It was best not to be in the locks at those moments.

One summer afternoon I was swimming in the lock quite near to the gate to the upper lock, with my back to the gate. The sides were about eight feet high, which meant I had nothing to grab hold of and had to swim to where the wall was lower.

One of the others decided it would be funny to open the gate without telling me. The first I knew about it was that my legs were being pulled out from under me, the current dragging me down. I fought with my arms to stay on the surface, but they quickly grew weak and tired. I was still in a part of the lock that was too high for me to be able to catch hold of anything or climb out. As I went under, fighting for breath, I imagined a newspaper headline: 'SCHOOLBOY DROWNS WHILE FRIENDS LOOK ON'. I pictured how Pauline and Dad would take the news and I imagined the school assembly with the headmaster breaking the news to the rest of the school, warning them of the dangers of swimming in the canal. They say your whole life flashes in front of your eyes at moments like that, but I seemed to be seeing the future.

Realising I was indeed drowning, I knew I had to make a decision whether to give in immediately or fight back. I felt a sudden surge of strength in my arms and managed to struggle back to the surface. I shouted for help, thrashing around to try to stay up and resist the currents that were pulling me back under. I wanted to live. The others, who saw no danger, laughed at my antics – I was always the one trying to get laughs out of every situation – apart from Arnie, who, seeing I was serious, dived into the lock and headed towards me. I felt him grabbing hold of me and together we swam to safety.

Trembling all over, I eventually pulled myself out onto dry land and spent a few minutes gasping for air. I knew that I owed my life to Arnie but neither of us said anything about it.

I realised that day that however bad things might have been in my life, I still didn't want to die, even when the way out was made to seem so easy. I had, it seemed, a strong instinct for survival.

chapter eight

the bloke
in the pub

At school I'd noticed a new girl in the year below us who seemed to be looking at me a lot. I had never imagined that any girl would be interested in someone as ugly as me, but it seemed possible that this one might be willing to be my girlfriend. Her family lived close to our house and I noticed her going past to visit them quite often. We started chatting at the front gate. Her name was Stephanie and she was a big-busted, dark-haired girl. She was a little on the large side and Pauline said she was a 'big-boned girl', whatever that meant. I fell for her very quickly and wanted to spend as much time with her as I possibly could. We would meet each morning on the walk to school and again on the way back. When teachers passed us in their cars I felt proud that they would be able to see I was just like other kids, that, contrary to everything I felt about myself, I was normal.

I was fifteen years old now and the day when I would actually be able to get away from home finally seemed to be coming within my reach. I felt that all my troubles were over. I was growing up at last and I didn't have to worry about how unattractive I was any more. I'd met the woman of my dreams and everything was going to be OK.

Stephanie's mum knew all about our mum because she lived on the same street as Auntie Vicky, so the subject was carefully avoided and I didn't have to provide any explanations about my family background.

If I thought it was all going to be smooth sailing from then on, however, I was wrong. Like most girls of that age, Stephanie was not sure that she wanted to settle down with the first boyfriend she had. I may have scared her with my intensity because after only a few months she started messing me around for no good reason that I could see. When I went to visit her she would tell me she no longer wanted to see me and I would end up standing forlornly in her garden, waiting for her to show herself at the window. I would write 'I love you' in the air with my finger, trying to show how strongly I felt about her. I wanted to feel safe and I guess she was looking for something a bit more exciting. She wanted to play games while I was terrified that if I lost her there would be no one else on the entire planet who would ever find me attractive again. This, it seemed to me, was my one and only chance of being loved and I couldn't understand why she was treating me the way she was.

A few days after each break-up she would tell me she wanted me back again and I would go running back. Her parents must have been worried about her going steady so young and when I bought her a dress ring with the money from my milk round, her mum panicked, thinking it might be an engagement ring, and told Stephanie to end the relationship.

My heart was broken. I'd just wanted to show her how much I thought of her. I cried my eyes out and begged Pauline to go to Stephanie's mum and talk to her. She very sweetly agreed to do her best on my behalf, but she wasn't even allowed past the doorstep. I took the ring back to the shop, but they wouldn't give me my money back, just a credit note. A few days later Stephanie told me her mum had changed her mind and she could see me again.

As my relationship with Stephanie developed, I spent less and less time with the gang. Sometimes I would stay over at her house for the whole weekend, sleeping on a camp bed. I loved being there because her parents seemed so normal and I could pretend her mum, with her warm, clean house, was mine too.

When George Oldfield, the former assistant chief constable on the Ripper case, died, the papers reported it with yet another outing of Sutcliffe's picture. One day, I vowed to myself, I was going to write to the *Yorkshire Post* and tell them what I thought of their editorial policies.

One of our cousins celebrated his twenty-first birthday in a nightclub in Leeds in the year that I was fifteen. I discovered later that it was the same place that Mum had visited on the night she was murdered – the Room at the Top. It was called something different by then. It was impossible to know if anyone was aware of the significance of the place because no one in the family ever talked about what had happened.

I was not used to drinking, apart from swigging cider from a bottle when I was walking around the streets with the other boys, but Dad said I could, as it was a family celebration. I hung round with another of my cousins, Patrick, both of us feeling very grown up. As the evening wore on, a man unconnected to our family offered to buy us drinks, obviously realising we were too young to go to the bar for ourselves. After a while he asked us if we wanted to go to a pub across the road.

'I'm going to stay here,' Patrick said, but I agreed to go. Why not? I thought. It wasn't every day that a grown-up was willing to buy me drinks like this. It felt good to be being treated like an equal, as if he wanted to be my mate.

'It's actually getting a bit late for the pub,' he said, looking at his watch as we came out of the club. 'They'll be closing soon. But I'm the landlord of another pub in Middleton. If we went there we could have as much beer as we wanted.'

My head was already spinning from the amount of drink I'd consumed and I had no idea what time it was. Had anyone even seen me leave the club? No one had said anything as we had left. Since I couldn't make any decisions for myself I shrugged my agreement. He hailed a taxi and we travelled across town to the Middleton area. I was too drunk to be able to work out the route we were taking. None of the streets looked familiar, but the driver and my new friend both seemed to know where they were going, so I wasn't worried.

When we arrived at the pub it was obviously closed, which made me confused, but when he got out his keys and opened the door I felt relieved that he was telling the truth about being the landlord and felt that I was in safe hands. I didn't give a second thought to how I would get back to the party later. He let us in, locking the door behind us to make sure no one else thought the pub was open for business, and switched on all the lights.

'I'll get you a pint,' he said, going behind the bar.

I spotted a pool table and wandered over to rack up the balls. As I tried to make sense of their colours and positions I realised I was very drunk indeed. The balls were going off in every direction and I couldn't get my brain to focus on what I should be doing to control them.

'Stand still for a minute,' my new friend said, coming over from the bar to join me. I wasn't sure what he meant but then nothing much was making sense, so I straightened up and tried not to sway.

Crouching down in front of me, he unzipped my fly. As my brain took in what was happening I froze, time grinding to a halt. I was unable to think of the appropriate words to stop him. He took my penis out, leaned forward and put it into his mouth. It was a sensation I'd never experienced before, even from a woman, and to my horror my penis started to respond to it, even though I knew it was wrong and shouldn't be happening. The panic almost sobered me. I realised I was trapped. I was locked inside a pub with a man who was much older and stronger than me. If I made a mistake now and he became angry I could be in real trouble, but I had to find a way to stop what was happening. I'd read so many stories over the years of young boys who'd been abducted, their bodies turning up weeks or months later. This was the sort of situation Mum had got herself into and now I was doing the same thing. I'd brought this on myself. I forced myself to think straight. I had to stop him, but at the same time keep him on my side.

'Can we stop now?' I asked politely, trying desperately not to sound angry. How would a man think about sex? I wondered. 'Why don't we go and find a prostitute?' I suggested, hoping that I sounded like I knew what I was talking about. 'Then we can both have fun with her.' It was all I could think of to get out of the pub and this situation.

'OK,' he said. 'Let's do that.'

I felt relieved, but unsure what was going to happen as we came out of the pub and he led me to his caravanette. I still felt horribly uneasy at what was going on, but at least he didn't seem to be angry or aggressive. We climbed in and he turned the key, but nothing happened. He tried a few more times, but still nothing.

'It's no good,' he said eventually. 'Let's go back inside and have another drink.'

I didn't like the idea of going back into the building, but I couldn't think what else to do. There was no one else on the streets who I could turn to for help and I had no idea where I was or how to get back to my part of town. I didn't have any money on me to pay for a taxi, even if I'd known where to go to look for one.

'Do you know the numbers of any girls we could call?' I asked as we went back inside, desperate to keep his mind off the possibility of using my body to relieve himself. He locked the door again and began to get angry, as if he'd worked out what I was trying to do and had had enough of it. My heart was pounding now. If I didn't do something quickly I was going to end up getting badly hurt. Even though I was still drunk the adrenalin was racing through my system. Grabbing a bar stool, I jumped onto a bench and started to shout, threatening to throw the stool through the window and jump through the broken glass. I meant it; I would rather have taken my chances on the broken glass that have let him have his way with me.

He must have realised that he wasn't going to be able to win me round or intimidate me. Maybe my shouting worried him, fearing it would attract someone outside, because he unlocked the main doors and I made a run for it, half expecting him to follow me as I stumbled out into the cold night air, sobbing with a mixture of fear and relief.

I tried to think what I should do next. Through my alcohol- and adrenalin-befuddled brain I remembered Dad telling us that if we ever got ourselves into a dangerous situation like this we should go to the nearest door and ask for help.

I ran up to the house next to the pub. The windows were all dark, which meant there was either no one in or they were safely in bed. No lights came on as I hammered on the door, terrified that the man in the pub would hear the noise I was making and come after me to shut me up.

After what seemed an eternity I gave up and ran to the next door, still crying uncontrollably. The windows were dark here as well, but this time a light went on as I banged and shouted. Someone came to the window.

'What do you want?' a voice demanded.

I tried to force the words out but they couldn't get past the sobs. My brain was muddled and I just sounded like an incoherent drunk.

'Bugger off home!' the voice said, and the window slammed shut.

The man hadn't come out after me so my panic began to subside, replaced by a feeling of helplessness as I walked away into the night. After about half an hour I came across a bus shelter and decided to sit down and try to get some sleep to clear my head. As the panic subsided and I started to shiver I realised how cold it was. I had nothing with which to cover myself, still being in my party clothes. The streets all around were empty and silent and I just wanted to be home and in my bed. Although I knew I was in Middleton I had no idea which direction I should head in to get home.

I finally managed to doze off and was woken at five-thirty by a bus pulling into the shelter with a hiss of brakes and clunking of doors. My head was thumping and I could smell the dried sweat of the previous night on my clothes.

'Do you want to get on?' the driver shouted to me.

'I don't know where I am,' I told him.

'Where do you live?' he asked. I told him. 'Get on then,' he said. 'I'll take you down to the centre of town and then you can get another bus to take you home from there.'

The driver dropped me in the city centre and I waited amongst the early morning street cleaners for the bus that would take me home. I was convinced they all knew exactly what had happened to me and I felt ashamed of myself. By the time the bus came it was all I could do to fight back the tears. I'd actually allowed a man to perform oral sex on me. I was confused, disgusted and embarrassed. Why had I got an erection so easily? Did this mean that I was gay? Had my whole relationship with Stephanie been a lie from the start? It was something that had never occurred to me before.

I never told a soul about what had happened in the Middleton pub, pushing the memory to the back of my mind where it festered.

In December of that year, 1985, Doreen Hill, whose daughter had been Sutcliffe's last victim, had her attempt to sue the West Yorkshire Police for negligence thrown out. The judge said that the police could not be held responsible for every unaccompanied female in the area who might become the victim of a crime. And the papers brought out every last detail of the saga yet again with Mum's photo staring out at all the ignorant, comfortable, happy people yawning and eating their breakfasts.

chapter nine

growing pains

When Sonia left school, the staff at the home arranged for her to have a flat a few streets away from our house, which meant I could go round and see her in the evenings. I felt so happy that she was in charge of her own destiny and becoming an independent adult. I couldn't wait to be in the same position myself.

She started a government training scheme, which gave her £27 a week to learn typing and parenting skills and anything else they could think of. She made a friend on the course, Maria, who became her flatmate, and she took a fancy to a boy called Andy, who looked like the lead singer of UB40. They started going out and when Sonia met his parents she thought that all her troubles were over. His family were the complete opposite to ours - loving, stable and living in a clean, tidy, warm, comfortable home. Andy made her feel wanted and she longed to be with him all the time.

At sixteen the time was drawing near when I would be able to leave school if I wanted to, and I certainly did. I had no wish to prolong my childhood for a moment longer than necessary. I was certain that the freedom of adulthood would be a thousand times more enjoyable than what had happened before. If I left school I would be able to get a job, earn some money and become independent of my family. The headmaster called me down to his office to ask if I'd got any thoughts on what I wanted to do at the end of the year.

'I just want to leave school and start trying to build a life for myself,' I told him.

I didn't have the slightest idea what I was going to do, and I certainly hadn't considered the possibility to going to university. The subject of further education simply never came up at home. Dad and Pauline didn't really care what I did and gave me no advice or encouragement, just assuming that I would sort it out for myself. Dad had always drifted from one job to another, often ending up being sacked for not turning up on a Monday morning after a weekend bender. He wouldn't have known where to start in making a career plan. Watching him and seeing his mistakes made me all the more determined never to miss a day's work if I could help it. I resolved to make something of my life, despite the bad start.

At the beginning of 1986 I decided it was time to embark on my adult life, and get myself out of the house as quickly as possible. I decided I would become what was called an 'Easter

Leaver', and just go back in for the examinations in the summer. Paper qualifications didn't seem that important to me. I just wanted to get some experience in the workplace and show a boss what I was capable of doing. I applied for a job in the press-room of a men's trouser factory. It was a big mill, on four floors, and my job involved pressing and dispatching the trousers once they'd been made, for which I was to be paid an unbelievable £120 a week, as long as I went in on Saturday mornings as well. Since Pauline only asked me to provide £15 a week towards my board I was rich. The company sent me to college one day a week, because then they could claim something towards my wages from the government. I thought it might be a fiddle the company was operating, since everyone else in the class was on a youth training scheme. Many of them were young girls work-ing as machinists in one of the many local tailoring companies and we got on really well.

When we were chatting one day during a break a group of them told me they were from the Middleton area. My stomach turned over at the mention of the name and all the memories of the bloke in the pub came flooding back. I tried to keep calm and asked casually if they knew the pubs in the area. I think at the back of my mind I rather hoped to find out where the pub was so that I could go back one day and exact some sort of revenge.

'I went to one once,' I said. 'It was a detached building with a big door at the front.'

'You mean the Middleton Arms,' one of them exclaimed.

'The landlord there's well known for messing around with young boys.'

'Has he messed you around?' another asked.

'No,' I lied, hoping I wasn't blushing. 'I just went there once with a friend and they served us even though we were underage.'

Just remembering the incident made me feel dirty and guilty, as if I'd done something wrong. I went back to work as quickly as possible and, to my relief, none of the girls ever mentioned the conversation again.

My status at home changed overnight. I was no longer one of the children. I was now an adult wage-earner. Pauline even began serving me the same food as Dad, giving me things like fried chicken legs with chips and peas. I felt I was finally leaving my childhood behind.

Stephanie and I had been having sex for a few months by then, but it was always hard to find places to go and once, when I knew Dad and Pauline were out, a few hours in an empty house were too tempting to resist. Pauline, however, came back sooner than I'd expected and it was obvious what had been going on from the flustered state we were in. When Dad got home it didn't take Pauline long to furnish him with the details. He didn't say anything for a while, leaving me to stew in my own embarrassment, but when he did finally bring it up he was furious, firstly because Stephanie was only fifteen and secondly because we'd done it in his house.

By then I'd already made some enquiries about renting a bedsit in order to get out of the house. It was going to cost me a great deal more than the £15 that Pauline was charging me, but I thought that perhaps I could go and live with Sonia and Maria until I sorted myself out. I just needed an excuse, and he'd given me one. I got my things together, which didn't take long, and left Broadlea Street. It felt like shedding an old skin.

As I walked the half-mile or so to Sonia's I prayed that she would let me live with her and that I would be able to make a new start. I needn't have worried. She understood exactly how I felt and welcomed me with open arms. At last, after so many years, we were both away from Dad and back together, just as we had been when our lives had first started to go so badly wrong. We felt that all the hurt was behind us and we could face anything together if we had each other for support. We could watch television when we wanted, drink when we wanted, go out when we wanted, say what we wanted and, most importantly of all, be ourselves and be together.

We would glug wine brewed by a local guy that Dad and Pauline knew and the evenings were often long and drunken. Once her youth training scheme was over, Sonia would be in the flat during the day and would sometimes cook so that I had a hot dinner waiting for me when I got home from the trouser factory. It wasn't a perfect situation because of the lack of space. I slept on the sofa and couldn't get to sleep until everyone else had gone to bed, which meant I was tired at work and pretty ratty by the time I came home. However, it was still pretty bloody good compared to everything that had gone before. Work was going well, I was making new friends and I had money in my pocket. Things hadn't been very smooth between Stephanie and me, but it didn't seem quite so important when the rest of my life was going so well. Then, two years after we first started going out, Stephanie dropped her bombshell.

'I've missed my period,' she announced, and I literally felt myself running cold with fear. I'd just started to get my life together and be happy for the first time ever and I'd managed to get an underage girl pregnant. Stephanie was still falling in and out of love with me at an alarming rate, and now we were supposed to be having a child together. I felt sick with horror. A wage of £120 a week might seem a lot for a single man with no responsibilities; it would be a very different matter if it had to support three of us. Where would we live? How would we survive? After just a few months of freedom we would be trapped in poverty for ever, just like my parents, and I would never be able to escape.

'You need to do a test before we tell anyone,' I told her. 'I'll go and buy a kit.'

I bought the pregnancy test and took it home to study the instructions. Stephanie filled a urine sample bottle in the morning and brought it round to the flat in the evening on her way home. I poured some of the urine into the tester tube, hardly able to stop my hand from shaking with nerves. I re-read the instructions. If a red dot appeared in the small, light-coloured pad after an hour then the result was positive. Eventually the minutes had all drained away and there it was, a perfectly formed red dot. I could hardly breathe as I tried to force myself to be calm.

I went to Stephanie's house at once and we walked round and round the streets as we talked. Stephanie cried. I tried to comfort her and assure her that I would stand by her and the baby whatever happened.

Eventually I walked her back home and we embraced tearfully on the back doorstep. She went in and I trudged home alone, not knowing who to ask for help. Sonia was still out somewhere when I got back to the flat and I fell asleep on the sofa.

The next day after work I rang Stephanie.

Her dad answered the phone. 'Stephanie doesn't want to see you any more,' he told me.

We were going to have a baby together and she didn't want to see me? Did her parents know about the baby? I couldn't bring myself to ask, but I couldn't bear the thought of being so brutally excluded.

'Can I just have a quick word with her?' I asked, shocked, but she wouldn't come to the phone.

Deciding that I had to let her parents know what was going on, I grabbed the positive pregnancy test and put it in a brown paper bag. My heart was racing as I rehearsed all the things I wanted to say. I was now more upset about her dumping me again than I was about the pregnancy.

Stephanie's dad answered the door, which was a relief. I much preferred dealing with him than with her mum, who was the tough one of the family.

'Can I see Stephanie?' I asked.

'She's not going to speak to you,' he said. 'She doesn't want to see you again.'

She obviously hadn't told them about the pregnancy, but they needed to know now in case there was going to be a termination. I gave him the brown bag.

'In that case,' I said, 'this is for Stephanie's mum.'

I walked away feeling I'd done the responsible thing, but I also felt an enormous rage towards Stephanie for dumping me in such a cruel manner when I'd been willing to stand by her.

Wandering the streets, trying to make sense of it all, I bumped into Stephanie and her two older sisters, who had been sent out to find me because their mum wanted to 'have a word'.

Stephanie ran upstairs to her bedroom and the sisters frog-marched me into the living room where their mum was waiting. She ranted and raved at me, refusing to stop shouting until she was certain I understood exactly what a disgusting creature I was.

'For your information,' she spat, 'Stephanie has started her period now and wasn't pregnant at all.'

I was stunned. Why hadn't Stephanie told me that herself?

'And if you ever lay a finger on her again I will be informing the police and you'll be arrested for having sex with a minor.'

When I finally staggered out of the house, mentally battered if not physically, I also felt relieved. I wasn't going to have to deal with the responsibility of another life, at least not yet. It was only later I discovered that for the pregnancy kit to be accurate I should have tested the urine within a few minutes of Stephanie producing it. By leaving it several hours we'd achieved an entirely wrong result.

I didn't contact Stephanie again.

chapter ten

finding mum
and losing sonia

While I was staying with Sonia we decided to contact some of Mum's family in Inverness. We hadn't seen any of them since she died, apart from the uncles who had moved down to Leeds at the same time as Mum in the early seventies. Dad had never let us keep in touch with them while we were living with him. We were so excited at the thought of meeting our grandma after such a long time, since she was the closest we were ever going to get to Mum herself.

When we arrived at Inverness bus station we were met by a couple of uncles who made us feel very welcome and special. We went first to one of our aunts, who lived in a private house on the outskirts of the city. Like so many other homes that we visited, we were struck by how spotless it was. I longed to live in a house like this, somewhere calm, ordered and cared for. This was how I wanted to live one day. I didn't know how I was going to achieve it with no education or skills, but I intended to keep working at it until one day I had a home like this of my own, somewhere where I could feel safe and secure and plan my life in an orderly fashion. It was wonderful to find something I wanted to aim for, like a good secret, but it was frustrating not to be able to see a path to achieving it. For a week we were taken from one house to another, meeting relatives and being treated like visiting royalty.

When we were taken to our grandma's house I was disappointed not to be overwhelmed by a feeling of love. She bore no resemblance to my mother. She was simply an elderly lady, who smoked and had a lot to say for herself. Perhaps it was hard for her to be reminded of Mum after so many years of trying to live with the truth of what happened on the night she died. Maybe she had seen Mum described as a prostitute so many times in the press that she'd begun to wonder if it was true. Or there might have been something else in the past between them that we knew nothing about. Perhaps it was just that too much time had elapsed and none of us knew how to bridge the gap.

At the end of the week we returned to Leeds, promising everyone that we would stay in touch, but it was many years before we made contact again.

Dad had never told any of us where Mum was buried, but one afternoon, on the way to a pub football match, we passed a cemetery with big, wrought-iron gates, and I heard him tell one of his friends that Mum was laid to rest there. I didn't say anything but I stored the information and decided it was time I paid her a visit. I wanted to say goodbye. The next day I made my way to the wrought-iron gates. I'd never visited anyone's grave before.

There seemed to be stones and monuments stretching away as far as the eye could see in every direction, hundreds of them, and I had no idea where to begin. There was nothing for it but to start walking down the first path I came to. Some of the gravestones had obviously been there for a hundred years while others looked brand new. For some reason I didn't stop to read any of the inscriptions. It was as if I knew none was Mum's. After about twenty-five yards I stopped and looked to the right where there was another row of stones set back from the edge of the gravel road, which was just wide enough for a hearse to bring bodies to their burial. I stepped up onto the grass and walked along this row and the first name that swam into focus before me was Wilma McCann. It was as if I had known where she was all along.

My heart was thumping uncontrollably as I drew closer. I was actually standing next to all that was left of my mum for the first time since she was taken from me ten years previously. I stood very still, unsure how I should be feeling or what I should be doing. I tried to remember the very last time that I'd seen her before she vanished from our lives, but I couldn't. I began to cry then, the tears stopping and starting of their own volition, as if

I had no control over them or the emotions that were bubbling up behind them and struggling to get free of the barriers I'd erected over the years to avoid being hurt.

I wondered how things would have been different if she hadn't met Peter Sutcliffe that night. I knew we wouldn't have been any better off financially, and there would always have been rows and dramas as boyfriends came and went, but our childhoods would have been filled with her love and that would have made everything different. I realised I'd been longing for love ever since that day and not receiving it from Mum for all those years was what had made me different from other children, not the freckles and the ginger hair or the jumble sale clothes. I saw the world differently because I would never know what a mother's love felt like. Dad wouldn't have wanted to see me cry like that. He would have wanted me to be stronger than the girls, but I knew that inside I was just as fragile and damaged as they were. There was no one else in that graveyard to see me break down or tell me not to be a crybaby. As I stood there, heaving with grief, I tried to make sense of everything that had happened to bring me to that place. For the first time I understood how everything is connected and how one action has a knock-on effect, like the ripples on the surface of a pond when you throw a stone into the centre of still waters. I knew then that the ripples caused by the murder of my mother would be felt by my children and their children and so on. I wondered where I would end up.

* * *

The cramped conditions in the flat were now fraying our nerves, Sonia hadn't managed to find job, and she and I were starting to have arguments in the evenings. We always had bickered, in the normal way that brothers and sisters do. Usually it was just a case of hurling abuse at one another, but one evening, the resentment that had been building burst out and Sonia hurled a cup of scalding tea over my stomach. My temper exploded and I dragged her to the sofa and sat on top of her, shouting furiously. At this point Maria decided to intervene on her friend's behalf and jumped on my back, trying to drag me off.

'Get out of my house!' Sonia screamed, and all the security I'd been feeling since moving in with her disappeared in an instant. If I left the flat there was only one place I could go at such short notice, and that was back to Dad's.

I climbed off her and went into the bathroom to pour cold water on my burns while Sonia lay on the sofa, crying. I knew I'd gone too far and had behaved like Dad and Keith and all the other men who resorted to violence when they couldn't cope with their anger. The pain of knowing that was worse than the burns.

I packed up my things in a daze, unable to believe what Sonia and I had just done to each other, or to see a way back to where we were before. Sonia was the most important person in the world to me, and I was pretty sure the feeling was mutual, but I'd messed it up, at least for the moment.

At that time of day Dad would be in his local pub, which was only a hundred yards away from the flat. I walked slowly,

dragging my feet, hoping that some better alternative would occur to me before I reached the doors. It didn't. I stood outside for a while, not wanting to go in with all my worldly possessions and talk to him in front of his friends. There were a couple of kids playing in the car park and I sent one of them in to ask Dad to come out and talk to me. Dad appeared a few seconds later.

'Can I come back home?' I asked, sheepishly.

'OK,' he said, apparently not surprised or bothered by my sudden change of heart, and five minutes later I was back at Broadlea Street and unpacking my few possessions.

But things had changed between us. It wasn't that bad being in the house any more, at least not for me. It was as if Dad and I had moved on to a new place in our relationship now that I was a working man, and he didn't try to dominate or control me. The days stretched into weeks and I stayed on. Dad would often still become drunk and abusive, but nowhere near as badly as when we were little. He seemed to be mellowing towards me with age and I had grown so used to the sound of his bitterness I hardly heard it any more.

At the end of the summer it was Angela's turn to start high school. The change seemed to affect her badly and she became more and more defiant, staying out later and later and constantly being grounded. I didn't want to get involved. I was just relieved that it wasn't me at the centre of the endless rows and stayed out of the house as much as I could.

Things grew worse between them, and Angela began not coming home for a couple of days at a time, just like Sonia had done at her age. A couple of times the police were called and they brought her home. In the end Social Services agreed it would be in her best interests to be taken into care and both Dad and Angela were obviously relieved. The shape of the household was changing now. Donna and I were the only members of Mum's family left at home, outnumbered by Dad, Pauline, Cheryl, who was eleven, and Daniel aged two.

Sonia's eighteenth birthday came and went and we still hadn't managed to patch up our differences. Then it was Angela's fourteenth birthday and we didn't hear anything from her either. I used to enjoy birthdays when I was young because it always meant we were guaranteed to get at least one present. Now I could see my seventeenth approaching and I knew it wasn't going to be the same.

With Stephanie out of my life, my school friends grown up and moved away, and no Sonia, my life took on a new shape. After work on a Friday lunchtime I would go to the pub with friends from the factory and drink for a couple of hours. When the pub closed at three we would make our way to the local gambling arcade where no one would bother to ask our ages. Once we'd lost as much as we could afford we would wait for the pubs to open again at five, sometimes going home to get changed before meeting up again to make a night of it. None of the other guys seemed to have any trouble chatting up girls, whereas I was terrified of approaching them, certain I would be laughed at. Why would anyone be interested in someone like me who had nothing to offer them? I felt like a leper and an outsider.

After a while, Sonia and I started talking again whenever we bumped into one another on the estate. During one of these casual chats she told me she and Andy were going to have a baby and I was about to become an uncle for the first time. She was so happy about it I felt overjoyed. At last she was going to have a family of her own and I was sure that she would be a wonderful mother, having had so much practice looking after the rest of us when we were little. It looked as if she was really sorting out her life and finding some stability for the first time. I was aware that she and Andy argued a lot, but I guessed all young couples went through that stage and that they would settle down once the baby had arrived and they knew where they stood. As the months passed, however, and Sonia and I grew closer as the bump swelled in her stomach, I realised that it was unlikely they were going to be living together by the time the baby arrived. I was disappointed for Sonia, especially when she told me that Andy hadn't even told his parents about the baby. It looked as if this relationship was going to bring no more stability to the family than any that had gone before.

The ghosts from our past continued to haunt us both as we tried to get on with our lives. A new Ripper book had appeared on the market called *The Street Cleaner*. I found the title deeply offensive, since it implied that Mum and all the other victims had been rubbish that Sutcliffe had 'cleaned' off the street. The newspapers came up with another Sutcliffe story about how his house was coming up for sale and a proportion of the proceeds would be used to pay off some of the claims against him for damages. His face was back on the front page, no doubt selling thousands of extra copies.

In the New Year a Sunday newspaper ran another story about the hoax tapes, claiming they'd been made by a disgruntled policeman. I didn't bother to read the story. I didn't care. None of it was ever going to bring Mum back to us. A few months later the whole story had been proved untrue, no evidence having been found.

Sonia was looking forward to the baby arriving, even if she wasn't going to have Andy there to help her as she'd hoped. It was going to give her someone to love and look after. Leanne was born on 22 February 1987 with no problems and was a real credit to Sonia, a beautiful, healthy baby.

Donna followed the family tradition of deciding she couldn't stand Dad a moment longer and went to live in a young person's hostel about a mile from the centre of the city, leaving me as the only one of Mum's children still at home with Dad. When Mum had died everyone had been so anxious to keep us together and Dad had failed miserably. He told the world that my three sisters were 'trouble', that they'd 'gone off the rails' and that them leaving home was nothing to do with him.

Since my relationship with Stephanie had ended I hadn't met anyone else that I could be faithful to and I was falling into bed with just about anyone who was willing and who I didn't have to chat up, finding some temporary comfort in sex but none of the stability or love that I craved so deeply. I went from one relationship to another; often ending up in bed with girls I knew nothing at all about.

Then, when I was seventeen, a young girl called Debbie joined the factory where I worked and it wasn't long before one of the girls told me that Debbie fancied me. I was thrilled by the compliment and even more excited when she asked if I wanted to go for a drink. Before long we were seeing each other almost every night. We would babysit together for one of her older friends and then sleep over at the house.

On one occasion, we were woken in the middle of the night by some gypsy who'd been brought home by the friend, and we were kicked out of the house with nowhere to go. I never took girls home after the Stephanie incident, being embarrassed by the way Dad behaved, but standing in the dark and cold that night we didn't seem to have any option.

Once we got there I crept into Pauline's bedroom and explained the situation, not sure how she would react. 'Do you mind if we sleep in my bed?' I asked.

'OK,' she said, probably impatient to get back to sleep herself.

When we woke up in the morning I could hear Dad and Pauline downstairs. Neither of us was too keen to get out of bed. I felt pleased that Pauline had treated me in such an adult way the night before, but I was still not sure what sort of reception we would get when we went downstairs.

Eventually we couldn't wait any longer and I got up. I managed to get Pauline on her own while Dad was organising his breakfast in the kitchen. The aroma of frying bacon was filling the house.

'Is everything OK with Dad?' I asked.

'It's fine,' she said. 'Get Debbie up and come down for some breakfast.'

I took Debbie into the kitchen, dreading what sort of reception might be waiting for us, but Dad just asked if we wanted bacon sandwiches. Pauline joined us and we had breakfast together like four adults.

The relationship went well for a while. I liked being with Debbie and respected the way she dealt with me when I was being difficult. After we'd been seeing each other for a few weeks we were invited to the wedding of one of my cousins. It was being held on the same day that Madonna was coming to Leeds for the opening concert of the European leg of her world tour, so there were a lot of crowds around the streets and a heavy police presence in case of any trouble. It was the middle of August and the weather was beautiful.

The ceremony was held at the registry office in the town centre and all the family were there. After the signing of the register we headed for the reception in the function room of a sporting club. I felt very proud to be there, in front of all my family, with Debbie. I wanted them to see that I was worthy of having a proper relationship, although I doubt any of them gave the matter a second thought.

For the first couple of hours everyone had a nice time meeting people and quenching their thirst. Then the effects of the alcohol began to kick in and some sort of argument broke out near the bar, turning into a scuffle. It was nothing unusual but I was disappointed to see Dad in the middle of it all, although it did look as if he was trying to calm the situation down. A burly friend of one of the aggressors, however, thought Dad was interfering and the aggression levels rose a few degrees as the rest of the party watched anxiously from their seats around the room, hoping things wouldn't get out of control and spoil the party and wondering if it would be a good idea to leave before things turned really ugly.

Suddenly there were two men grappling with one another on the floor and women were screaming at them to stop. The landlord was obviously an old hand at this sort of thing. He rang the police, asked everyone to leave the premises and pulled the shutters down on the bar. We gathered up our things and made for the door, hanging around in the entrance hall, unsure what we should do next. A few minutes later the police arrived and an air of control smothered the place. They asked us all to leave the club and be on our way. No one made any protest; there was nothing much to stay for now anyway.

As we walked outside Debbie was rummaging in her bag. 'I've left my asthma inhaler in there,' she said. 'I think I put it on the seat.'

'I'll go back for it,' I told her.

The entrance was now filled with policemen and there was no way they were going to let anyone back in now they'd cleared the place. I calmly walked up to the officer who seemed to be in charge of the door and tried to explain the problem without sounding as if I'd been drinking. I didn't do a bad job, but there was still no way he was going to let me back in.

Someone else came up to ask another question and he turned away just far enough for me to be able to slip past his back. I grabbed the opportunity. But before I'd got more than one foot in the club, he spun round and gripped hold of the green shirt I'd bought specially for the occasion. He was a big man, well over six feet, and probably weighed about five stone more than me; I didn't stand a chance. He marched me force-fully down to the white police car parked on the steep hill outside. It felt as if my feet hadn't touched the ground. Two other officers waited by the car. My head smashed down onto the bonnet and I could feel the warmth of the engine underneath on my cheek. One of the other officers must have thought I looked like I was about to fight back because he pinned me down with his full weight on my back. Everything around seemed confused and noisy. A few seconds later the officer reappeared in my line of vision, having been hustled away by Dad. I was then bundled into the car by the original man, with my hands cuffed behind my back while the other two concentrated on restraining Dad.

Auntie Katherine then decided to wade into the fray in defence of her youngest brother and when Dad's brother, Patsy, also joined in, the police knew they had a situation on their hands that was close to getting out of control. I watched the scene unfolding from inside the police car, unable to move because of the cuffs, and within a few minutes the street was swarming with officers and dogs, who must have been diverted from patrolling the Madonna concert. A dozen or more police cars had poured in and it seemed to have had the right effect in calming down the rest of the family as they watched us being carted off.

As we drove away, I saw Debbie standing beside Pauline. She was holding up her inhaler.

We were taken to the local jail and Dad, Patsy and I were thrown into a communal cell with about fifty other drunks, most of whom had been arrested at the concert. Katherine was in the women's cell, which gradually filled up with drunks and prostitutes as the evening passed.

Although I was still only seventeen, I tried to play the adult. It was a laugh to start with, but as the night dragged on I started to become bored and cold. I lay down on the floor to try to get some sleep but it was hard because of all the drunken voices shouting around us. We were released the next morning and the following day we were bound over to keep the peace for twelve months.

At Christmas Pauline festooned the house with the same decorations she used every other year. She took great pride in dressing the Christmas tree with flashing lights and coloured tinsel. On the last day at work before the two-week seasonal shutdown everyone was talking about going out that evening and we set out straight from work in high spirits, looking forward to the holiday. After a while we all drifted off in separate ways and I ended up in a nightclub just a short distance from home. It was a popular place with locals because the dress codes were less strict than in the clubs in the centre of town, allowing customers to wear trainers and sports clothes. Every weekend there were fights there; some people didn't seem to think they'd had a good night out if it didn't end with a few punches being thrown, and at times it seemed as if half the club was 'battling', as they liked to call it. I decided to head home earlier than usual and as I came in through the kitchen door just after midnight I knew there was something going on.

I could hear Dad's voice coming from the front room with the vicious, arrogant tone that meant he was smashed on whisky. It wasn't his usual drunk voice; it was the one that made him sound evil and frightening, like a man who could lash out at the slightest thing.

'Where have you been?' he snarled, as I entered the room.

Pauline was sitting on the sofa looking uncomfortable and there was an almost empty bottle standing on the mantelpiece next to a half-full tumbler of neat whisky. I guessed that he'd come home drunk and had decided to keep going, which guaranteed that things were going to get nasty.

'I've been to the Bar-C,' I told him.

'You think you know how to have a good time,' he shouted. 'I'll show you how to have a good time.'

He pulled himself out of the chair and I thought he was suggesting we should go back to the club together.

'I'm going to bed,' I said, shaking my head, and went upstairs. I could hear Pauline trying to tell him that it wasn't a good idea to be thinking of going back out at this time of night. Then I heard him yelling and the crash of something being thrown across the room. I heard Pauline shouting his name and I ran back downstairs to check he wasn't hurting her.

Dad stormed out of the room and upstairs to bed as I came in. Pauline was sobbing and the Christmas tree with all its decorations was scattered across the room. As we started to clear up the mess we both knew that he was never going to change.

'You don't have to put up with this any more, you know,' I told her. 'You should get away from him as soon as possible.'

We waited until we could be sure he had fallen into a deep, drunken sleep before she went up to bed. The next day, while he was in the pub, she gathered together her things in black bin liners, a sadly familiar sight, and called for a taxi. She took Cheryl and Danny with her and the moment the taxi pulled away the house fell silent. Now it was just Dad and me left.

I had mixed feelings as I waited for him to come home that day. I knew he was going to be lost without Pauline, but I also knew that he'd brought it on himself. Every time this had happened before he'd promised to cut down on the drink, and had usually managed it for a while, but he always ended up going back to it.

'Where's your mum?' he asked when he eventually stumbled in through the door.

'She's left,' I said. 'She's gone to her mother's.'

To my surprise he didn't say much, just turned round and went back to the pub. I didn't bother to wait up for him and some hours later he woke me up.

'I can't sleep,' he said. 'Do you want to come downstairs for a chat?'

Reluctantly I got up and went down with him. Sitting there listening to him, I realised he truly didn't think he had done anything wrong and I felt very sorry for him. I eventually persuaded him to go to bed, but every evening over Christmas he would get me out of bed to talk over what had happened yet again. Mostly it was him talking and me listening, and I didn't mind too much to start with, but after a few weeks of going over and over the same ground it started to get to me. He kept telling me how he couldn't understand what he had done wrong or why Pauline had left him. No matter how many times I explained, he asked the same questions over and over again, as if he couldn't hear me. One night, when he was feeling particularly sorry for himself, he rang the local radio station in the early hours and asked them to play a dedication to Pauline: *'When will I see you again?'* He was missing her and hurting badly. He even seemed to be losing weight. He must have hoped that he would persuade her to come back like he always had before, but when he heard that she'd got a flat of her own, he knew that it was all over. He tried going on dates with a couple of other women over the next year, but the relationships didn't develop. He just wanted Pauline back.

He didn't stop drinking and now it made him even more miserable. One night he got so low he went out to the pigeon coop he'd built in the garden and set light to it, incinerating all the birds on a mad funeral pyre of old timber.

Pauline's flat was only a couple of miles from where Mum had been killed, but I wasn't going to let that stop me from visiting her. Our relationship had grown close over the years of living with Dad; we'd both suffered in very similar ways and had formed a bond as a result. Although I have referred to her as 'Pauline' in this book, to avoid confusion, I had grown used to calling her 'Mum' and was comfortable with it. She'd been the closest thing I'd had to a mother since the night of the murder.

Sonia's relationship with Andy was not going well and one night she rang me to confide that he'd started to be violent towards her. I was also having problems with my own relationship with Debbie. I was behaving terribly at times, which I was ashamed of but didn't seem to be able to do anything about.

One evening while we were out drinking in a pub in the city centre, for instance, I noticed a girl looking at me while Debbie's back was turned. I was like a dry sponge for any sort of attention from anyone and returned the girl's eye contact. When Debbie disappeared to the toilet I went over to the girl and started to talk to her. It was obvious that both of us were interested in one another but the moment I saw Debbie emerge from the toilet I moved away quickly. I knew that she'd seen what was happening from the look on her face.

Debbie picked up her glass as I rejoined her and took a sip from it, still staring furiously at me. I couldn't look her in the eye, gazing self-consciously around the room at everyone and everything except my girlfriend's face. I only realised the foolishness of this course when I felt the cold lager flowing over the top of my head. I should have kept my eye on her.

Anger now replaced guilt at this public humiliation and I grabbed her by the back of her dress and walked her purposefully to the door. I couldn't believe what she had just done to me. Both of us having had too much to drink, we argued so forcefully as we walked through the city centre that at one point two guys came over to ask Debbie if she was all right. Even more furious at the suggestion that my girlfriend needed protection from me, I swore at them and they started threatening me. I had just enough self-control left to realise that I was going to come off worse in any fight with these two and backed off, walking away with Debbie and continuing the argument all the way to her house. I knew I was in the wrong, but that knowledge just made me angrier and more aggressive. I was furious at the public humiliation she had visited on me, especially as I had deserved it.

Arguing in the cold night air, on top of the guilt, mixed with the humiliation, was fanning the flames of all my bottled-up and blocked emotions. I was becoming more and more angry and aggressive and less and less able to keep control. As we drew near to her house we passed a tree growing close to the pavement. I ripped off a long branch and swung it towards her, only missing by inches. Rightly incensed by this attack, Debbie shouted back even more angrily. I whipped her legs with the branch. The moment I'd done it I realised I'd gone too far and that there wasn't a single reason on earth why I should hurt her like that. She was entirely in the right, I was entirely in the wrong and I had now made things a hundred times worse.

After a few days of distance between us, and numerous grovelling phone calls from me, we were back together, but we would never be able to recapture the earlier happiness of the relationship. I'd introduced a note of instability and fear into it that I would never be able to fully exorcise. Things went from bad to worse between us and towards the end of the year we called it a day.

I went back to my old ways, recklessly sleeping with any girl who was willing. I also started another relationship with a girl at work, which ended abruptly when one of her friends saw me in a nightclub with someone else.

I left the factory and went to work for a direct sales company, knocking on doors and arranging appointments for their sales reps, who would then stitch up the unsuspecting householders. I did quite well there and enjoyed the challenge, but it was a commission-related job, and I didn't like the uncertainty of that.

Dad managed to get himself a girlfriend, which meant he was out a lot of the time, and I was often in the house on my own. Sometimes the only way I could tell he had been there at all would be when a shirt I'd neatly ironed in preparation for a night out would disappear. He was entirely oblivious to how much it annoyed me when he did things like that.

During the summer advertisements started appearing on television for a documentary titled *The Yorkshire Ripper Investigation*. I grew sick of watching them and made a point of being out of the house when the programme was broadcast. I don't know if Dad watched it. I was now eighteen years old and he still hadn't discussed the subject with me.

When Christmas came round again, with Pauline and the girls all gone, there were no decorations in the house and it brought home to me just how joyless my life had become. I didn't enjoy my job, I wasn't in a relationship and was going from one easy woman to another, constantly searching for something that loveless sex never provided. It was time to make a major change in my life.

chapter eleven
joining the army

At the beginning of 1989 I decided to join the Army. Dad seemed pleased, but it was Pauline who seemed proudest of me. Sonia told me she would miss me and Donna said that she was happy for me but I could tell it didn't mean much to her. I hadn't seen Angela for a while so I wasn't sure what she thought.

'From this moment onwards,' the sergeant informed me once I'd sworn my oaths, 'you are a soldier in the British Army and you must act like one. Don't advertise the fact that you're a soldier and watch yourself at all times.'

He gave me train tickets to Woolwich in London to start my twelve weeks' basic training. I had signed up for twelve years and was to join the Royal Artillery.

I said all my farewells over the next two weeks and on 21 March 1989 I left Leeds to start what I thought would be a new life. I believed that I would finally be able to shake off the unhappiness and insecurity of my past and begin again. It was to prove a hopeless fantasy.

There was no one at Leeds station to see me off as I boarded the train to leave. As I looked out of the carriage window at the empty platform outside, it seemed symbolic of how my life had been. Since Mum had died we had all been managing on our own.

Every gunner who has ever joined the Royal Artillery has carried out his basic training at the barracks in Woolwich. As we drove past the high, green-mesh perimeter fence in the minibus that had been sent to collect us, I felt thrilled to be amongst other guys who had decided to follow the same career. Most seemed younger than me, but I didn't think that would be a problem. Inside the fence were at least ten blocks, each two storeys high with row upon row of windows. I guessed we would be sharing rooms and hoped I'd be put with someone who would become a friend.

Two soldiers were guarding the entrance barrier as we turned in. One of them checked under the vehicle with a mirror on a long stick, then his colleague lifted up the barrier to let us pass. This is it, I thought, this is the start of my new life.

I was put into Marne troop and shown where I would be sleeping, along with a dozen other guys. As we grabbed a bed each and put away our belongings, we were told to be outside the gym in an hour in our PE kit.

The burly instructor who was waiting for us informed us we had a minute to run to the end of the road, round a pole and back again. About forty of us set off and it was soon easy to spot the athletes amongst us as they pulled ahead on the return journey. I made it in a minute, but there were a few unfit ones who didn't.

'That was bollocks!' the instructor roared. 'Again!'

We all set off again, this time a little faster.

'Fucking bollocks, what was that load of crap?' he bawled. 'You people at the front, is that how you'd behave on the battlefield, leaving the weaker ones behind if they were having trouble?'

We'd learned our first lesson. We were a team, working together, not competitors in a race. The quicker ones should have encouraged the slower ones so that everyone got round the pole and back in a minute.

'Do it again as a group,' he shouted, 'and if you fail again you'll be coming back this evening for some extra-curricular physical training.'

This time the faster ones ran behind the slower ones, shouting encouragement all the way, and the whole group was back within a minute.

Next we were on our way to the gym with instructors shouting and swearing at us as they ran us ragged. This was known as 'beasting' and once it was over we were marched back to our block with the bombardier whose job it was to turn us into soldiers. For five weeks there was going to be no escape; no phone calls, no visits, no television and no time to do anything on our own. Our time, waking or sleeping, was theirs. We learned how to dress properly, how to make a bed as skilfully as a hospital nurse, how to present our lockers for inspection and how to polish our boots. The only time we were allowed to leave the barracks was when we went on a run. I felt so proud when we went out, forty of us at a time, running in pairs with our feet hitting the ground in unison, particularly when groups of women wolf-whistled and shouted suggestive remarks. I was beginning to realise the power of a uniform.

The worst part of it all was a parade change, which meant being ordered, without notice, to be outside the block in one particular set of clothing within two minutes. Everyone would dive for their lockers, searching for the relevant items, running outside and standing to attention in neat rows. Someone would always let the troop down and we would all be punished by being ordered to change into another set of clothing. Parade changes could happen at eleven at night or ten in the morning and always resulted in our lockers being in a chaos that would take hours to restore to inspection condition. After a change we would be told that there would be an inspection in an hour's time and we soon realised that it was a deliberate attempt to break us. Sometimes we would be woken at midnight by having our beds flipped upside down while we slept by a bombardier who had had a few too many drinks in the bar.

We had to patrol the camp in pairs on twelve-hour shifts, each armed with a rifle and one with a radio contact to the guardhouse. It was intimidating to know you were the only line of defence between the attackers and your colleagues asleep in the barracks. It was also deadly boring. I preferred daytime guard duty on the front gate, being the first person to greet people on arrival, although it was more nerve-racking than night duty with so many people coming and going. You had to be careful to recognise any ranking officers as they expected a salute. For the first few weeks our tormentors treated us like the lowest form of life imaginable; just smiling as you lined up on the drill square could have you marched off and made to crouch down with your back against a wall in the heat of the afternoon sun, or marched round the drill square with your rifle above your head. You soon learned the hard way what you could and couldn't do.

I'd never had so many friends, all of us part of a team, each of us knowing the strengths and weaknesses of the others. When the bombardier allowed it in the evening I would write letters to Sonia, Pauline and Dad, trying to keep my family around me in any way I could. One of the highlights of the day was when the post was given out and it was the lads with girlfriends at home who received the most.

After five weeks, if we'd earned our pips, we were allowed to leave the barracks. We had to prove that we could march, stand to attention and salute an officer. We were given one chance and if we failed a second time we were not allowed past the gatehouse. I was relieved to pass the first time, along with my colleagues, and the first thing we did was head for the pub. With our newly shaved heads we stuck out like sore thumbs but the local population seemed used to it. At weekends we would travel around London, seeing the sights.

During one hot afternoon on guard duty, I spotted a young blonde girl heading for the gate with an *A to Z* in her hand. She asked me for directions, and as she seemed genuine, I took the book from her and found the street in the index. It soon dawned on me that she wasn't really interested in directions at all.

'I just wanted to talk to you,' she confessed finally, slipping a piece of paper into my hand with a phone number on it. 'Give me a call tonight if you can.'

That night, once we were allowed out, I rang the number and we agreed to meet near the barracks. When she turned up she'd brought a friend with her. We chatted for about half an hour and arranged to go out on Friday night. I said I'd bring someone for her friend. None of us had had any female company for weeks, so it wasn't hard to find someone willing to come out with me. Neither of us minded that the women obviously didn't care who turned up as long as they were soldiers. We had a great night on the town and ended up sitting on a bench by a fountain in a grass square in Woolwich town centre. After a while, the blonde and I sloped off into some nearby bushes. Standing, with our heads above the bushes, I simply unzipped my fly and lifted her short skirt up around her waist. I could even see people walking past. It was the start of a sexual adventure that I pursued throughout the rest of my time at Woolwich.

I invited everyone to my passing out parade, and set about making sure I was going to be fit enough to make the grade. I wanted all my sisters to be there, and Pauline and Dad, even though I knew it was going to be tense as they were no longer together. Pauline said she would drive down with Sonia and Andy and maybe Donna and Angela. Dad said he would make his own way down by coach.

The night before the parade we all went out and got pissed with the bombardiers, who'd become a great deal friendlier now their task was nearly over. The next morning we were woken at six by a conscientious bombardier who forced us all to stand in ice-cold showers for a full minute to ensure we were completely sobered up from the night before.

At eleven o'clock, standing on the parade ground in my brown uniform and peaked cap, I scoured the audience for my family. It was no good, I couldn't make out any of the faces without losing my concentration. The military band was playing and we marched to a couple of anthems, finishing with a salute to the officer who was to judge each of the four troops on their appearance and marching ability. Although I wanted to win as much as anyone else, I was just happy to be there and to know that I was finally going to be a soldier. We finished our marching and in good old-fashioned tradition threw our peaked caps in the air as the crowd cheered. It was over and I stood there, looking around me, elated. All I needed now was to know that my family had made it and then I saw Sonia walking towards me, then Pauline and Andy. But that was it. Angela and Donna hadn't made it and there was no sign of Dad.

All around me my colleagues were surrounded by their complete families, everyone hugging them and taking pictures, the families as proud as their sons, but my dad hadn't even bothered to turn up. I tried to hide my disappointment as I took my family round the barracks and showed them where everything was. It was a beautiful day and I saw other soldiers introducing their parents to their friends. I didn't bother as I felt my dysfunctional family was obvious for all to see.

As we walked from the gym to the block that we'd all shared for the last eight weeks I saw a figure in the distance being let through the entrance to the barracks. I recognised my father's walk. Where all the other guests had put on their best clothes and spruced themselves up in honour of their sons, Dad had chosen to wear denim jeans and a sweater.

'I missed the coach,' he said when he finally reached us. 'I had to thumb a lift down the M1.'

He stank of beer and I was disappointed in him. I suppose I should have been grateful that he had tried to get there at all, and I shouldn't have been surprised that he had failed when put to the test. But I still held out hopes that one day he wouldn't let me down, that he would be there for me when I needed him, showing me his approval and pride. The trouble with hanging on to hopes like this in the face of all the evidence is that you are likely to be continually disappointed.

Once I'd finished the tour we got all my things together and headed home to Leeds for a two-week leave. Dad shared the ride and to my surprise it was a high-spirited journey with a lot of jokes and laughter.

For the next two weeks I enjoyed the feeling of having spare money in my pocket and of holidaying with my family. Then it was back to Woolwich to learn one of three trades. Most of the men were to become gunners, learning how to carry and load shells, trajectory and basic gun drill. Others were given driving lessons and a licence and taught the basics of vehicle maintenance. I was told that, as I was one of the brighter ones, I would be a signaller, learning about basic radio communications and how to identify and use the different radios we might come across in the Army. I was flattered and excited by this, knowing that we would be treated with a little more respect than the gunnery students.

Due to shortages not everyone was placed in their local regiment and I was told I was going to the Cheshire 32 Heavy Regiment, based in Dortmund, Germany. Although I was happy to be going abroad, I was disappointed to be separated from the other Yorkshiremen who had become my friends during training. I said a final farewell to my blonde and headed up to King's Cross for the train back up to Leeds.

I spent as much time as possible with my family, basking in the knowledge that they were proud of me at last. Dad had a new girlfriend, a woman who'd been going out with a friend of mine a few months earlier. She seemed to be making him happy and I went drinking with him one afternoon in an attempt to mend some fences. I tried to keep up with him, drink for drink, since it seemed to be the only interest we had in common, but I finished the day throwing up on his girlfriend's living-room carpet.

Around this time Sonia Sutcliffe, the Ripper's wife, brought a libel action against *Private Eye* magazine and won £600,000 in damages. It was later reduced to £60,000, still enough to destroy the magazine. A fund was launched by the readers to raise the money. I was angry to see the story back on the front pages, and even angrier to think that Sonia Sutcliffe should receive such large sums of money when we had to struggle so hard just to survive.

chapter twelve

running amok in germany

The journey to Dortmund took all day and it was a little after midnight when I arrived at the camp that would be my home for the next few years. I was the only one joining the regiment that night and I felt suddenly friendless, with no one to turn to if I needed help of any sort. I was sharing a room with a large soldier called Thumper from the south coast. It wasn't hard to imagine how he'd earned the name. We spent the first night together in silence. I was too terrified to open my mouth.

The next morning I was given my first duty. I was told to make my way to the officers' mess with a fork and a sergeant would meet me there. In front of the mess was a large cobbled area about the size of two tennis courts. I was told to get down on my knees and remove all the moss that had built up over the previous few months. As I laboured through the morning I felt completely demoralised. Had I really signed up for twelve years of this?

After lunch I went back to my room to rest for an hour before afternoon parade. I was so tired I was afraid I would fall asleep and miss it, so I asked Thumper to wake me up if I dozed off. The next thing I knew it was half past two; Thumper had let me sleep on. I ran to the area I was supposed to be working on to be greeted by a furious sergeant. He screamed at me to report to the guardhouse at six, after my day's work was over. When I reported to the guardhouse I was told to brasso the gun that was on display in front of the building. It had started to rain and as soon as I'd finished one area the water would ruin it again. I was quickly learning that the only person I could trust was myself. When I wrote home a few days later I kept the bad parts of my new life to myself, not wanting anyone to worry.

As the other members of the regiment returned from Northern Ireland, there was a memorial service for one of their fellow gunners who'd been killed there a few weeks earlier. It had happened just outside Londonderry. When they found out that my name was McCann and that my dad was from that very town, I was immediately classed as the enemy, part of the movement that had killed their friend. They were mostly Scousers, which meant my Leeds background was also held against me. For most of them I was an outsider from the beginning and it was soon obvious that it was going to stay that way.

It didn't take long for me to find a German girlfriend. She approached me in a bar and took me back to her place. It felt strange not being able to communicate in the same language since I spoke no German and she spoke no English. We spent a lot of time with a phrase book, trying to construct some sort of conversation, which normally ended with '*Ich liebedick*' and us having sex. It went on for several weeks and I would stay at her house, returning to camp in time for breakfast. It was fun while it lasted. My next girlfriend did speak some English, which she'd learned from her previous boyfriend, a Scotsman. I found it funny to hear a German girl with a Scottish accent. Her name was Petra and she lived with her elderly mother, whose family were in East Germany and hadn't been able to see her for decades.

Being a signaller I was able to travel around in the warmth of an armoured vehicle rather than on the big artillery pieces, which were open-topped and afforded no shelter from the freezing winter weather. We positioned ourselves in ranges deep inside Germany and practised fighting an imaginary Russian army. At last I was a soldier, even if it was only on exercise.

Six months after arriving in Dortmund I was able to go home for a visit. It was only once I got back to Leeds that I realised how sad I was to have been away. Sonia had been contacted by a senior police officer who asked whether we would accept a gift from *Private Eye* magazine. Apparently there was some money left over from the fund after Mrs Sutcliffe had been paid off and the magazine staff wanted to donate it to families of the victims. Sonia had told him we would be happy to accept it and we speculated wildly as to how much it might be. It was the first time anyone in the outside world had ever acknowledged that we might have been damaged by what had happened to our mother and might appreciate some help. It was a good feeling.

It seemed that Andy had been spending a lot of time round at Sonia's flat, and had often babysat for Leanne when Sonia wanted to go out to her 'blues clubs', illegal drinking dens that sprang up all over Leeds, usually in the basements of people's houses. She would often not return home until eight or nine in the morning. It was all very reminiscent of how Mum used to behave.

When I did get back to Dortmund one of the other lads produced a magazine he'd brought with him from England.

'Are you one of the children in the Ripper case?' he wanted to know, waving the magazine at me.

I felt my stomach turn over. As if being an enemy Irishman wasn't enough, they were now going to discover every sordid detail of my mother's death. The magazine was a fortnightly publication called *The Murder Casebook*. This issue was featuring the Ripper story and Sonia's name was mentioned. The others had heard me talking about my sister and knew my name was McCann, so it wasn't hard for them to work out the rest. The nightmare had found me again.

I didn't deny it. I never had when people had asked me in the past. In a way I wanted people to know that it was my mum, to understand what I'd been through and what was going on inside my heart and my head. Dad and Pauline had never shown any interest in discussing it, so my sisters and I were all desperate, whether we knew it or not, to be understood.

All the details of the night my mother died were reprinted. The squalid scene had been painted so many times for every thrill-seeker to read, it seemed unbelievable that they would want to go over the whole thing again, just regurgitating the same stuff that had been in the papers a hundred times, replaying a scene that had been revolving around inside my head for years.

Surely everyone who wanted to know could now picture the lime-green car drawing into the nursery car park in the park behind our house near the Prince Philip playing fields with its lights out at two in the morning. They could imagine Mum falling out of the car, drunk, in her white trousers and the tight-fitting green jacket. The writer told how Sutcliffe claimed he had picked her up just a few minutes before as she thumbed a lift home, eating chips from a polystyrene tray. By the time she stumbled out of the car she was abusing him for his inability to make love to her and he was annoyed, claiming he had paid her £5 for this experience. He went back to the car, returning with a hammer, determined to silence her. He didn't kill her with the first blows to her head and she was still moving about on the grass, her trousers around her ankles, so he went back with a knife he had in the glove compartment. He stabbed wherever he thought it would finish her off, first her lungs, then her neck, then her chest and finally she stopped breathing. She lay dead as the night mist thickened around her and we slept a few hundred yards away. Sutcliffe drove home to his wife.

Those were the images that I still had to deal with every moment of my life.

I tried to convince myself that the others would soon forget about it.

The next day we were due to start an exercise and we set off to some isolated woods, chosen for the purpose. I found it impossible to think about anything other than the article. We arrived at the site in the evening and decided to find the nearest pub. I was the youngest and most junior in the party; the rest were officers and sergeants.

We reached a scenic little village and the officers were telling stories about the things they'd got up to when they first joined the Army: drinking, fighting, womanising. One of them talked about how he'd got into trouble for pinching a bike. We were all laughing, but even as I laughed I was still thinking about Mum, about that green car and that man.

Every head seemed to turn as we walked into the pub in the picturesque village. There were about a dozen locals and their faces lit up at the sight of uniforms. A couple of the officers were fluent in German and so we were able to talk to the other people there. I don't think I bought a single drink all evening; the local people insisted on paying for every round. The German beer was strong and I realised I was getting more drunk than was wise the night before an exercise. It seemed a good idea to get back to our camp in the woods to get some sleep while I could still walk. I said goodnight and made for the door.

It was January and the air outside was freezing. As I wandered down the main street of the village, past the neat, quiet, semi-detached houses, I realised the walk was going to take forever now I no longer had the distraction of the other men's conversation. I remembered the officer talking about pinching a bicycle and decided to have a go myself. I found myself still thinking about Peter Sutcliffe, and how he had left his mark on society. In some small, stupid way I suddenly wanted to do the same. I wanted to leave *my* mark on this peaceful village full of people who were so different from me and who had no idea what I'd been through. I wanted to take revenge on the world, as I'd planned so many times when I was a child.

Spotting a low extension on the back of one house, I strode through the hedge and took a short run up to it, jumped for the guttering, then pulling myself up and sitting there, like a cat, eyeing up the neighbourhood in search of my next target. I spotted a large decorative windmill in the next garden, reminding me of the one Dad had built for us with lolly sticks we'd collected. I ran across the roof and launched myself, just missing the hedge and rolling on the grass like a member of the Paras landing in enemy territory. By the time I reached the windmill a rage had taken over inside my head and I smashed my boot into the centre of the structure, pieces flying in every direction. I ran down the side of the house into the silent street, my progress illuminated by the orange streetlights. I felt free.

Outside another house with no gate or fence to negotiate, I spotted a brand-new moped on its stand, facing into the darkened garden. I'd never learned to hotwire a bike or a car, even though many of my friends had, but that didn't deter me. A sliver of light was escaping from between the downstairs curtains. Walking as quietly as my combat boots would allow, I took hold of the handlebars, lifting it up and back off its stand. I turned it round and pushed it into the street, surprised by its weight. The road had a slight slope and I faced the bike downwards. I leaned forward and pushed. I had no idea what I was doing, but I didn't care. Needless to say, the engine didn't start, but the moped still gathered speed, racing silently past the houses. I leaped onto it and rode it for as far as it would take me, not caring what would happen next. I imagined driving into a wall and wondered if the crash would release the fury building up inside my head. But eventually the bike wobbled to a halt and fell over with me underneath it, still clinging on to the handlebars. My combat helmet hit the ground with a loud crack. I lay still, trying to get my breath back as the silence returned.

Car lights turned into the end of the road and headed towards me. I didn't move and the driver stopped a few yards away. He opened his door, not turning off the engine. I managed to raise myself a few inches and gave him the thumbs up as he walked towards me with a puzzled look on his face.

'OK?' he asked.

'*Ja*,' I replied. 'OK.'

He got back into the car, reversed to the bottom of the street, did a three-point turn and headed in the opposite direction. I extricated myself from the moped and looked around to see if I had attracted any attention from any of the houses. There was still no movement or sign of life anywhere. I walked in the same direction as the car, keen to get away from the scene of the crime.

I turned into another, identical street and immediately saw a black double-garage door standing slightly ajar. No one back home in Leeds would ever have left a door open like this; these people were asking for trouble. Inside, illuminated by a bright moon, I found a dark saloon car crammed into a small space. The walls were lined with narrow shelves containing everything a DIY enthusiast could need. There was a drill, a sander, tins of paint and other containers where I could only guess at the contents. I picked up a small, dark tin, unscrewed the cap and sniffed, quickly jerking my head back from the acrid smell. I didn't know what it was, but it smelled dangerous, so I emptied it over the gleaming paintwork of the car.

I left the garage as quickly as possible and walked past a few more houses before choosing my next victim, a garden lined by a waist-high wood-panelled fence. I booted the fence like I was taking a penalty kick and my foot went straight through the panel.

I made my way on down the street until I found another unlocked garage door. Inside was a bicycle. Remembering the officer's story about stealing a bike, I wheeled it away from the house, jumped on and pedalled back to the woods. Throwing the bike aside, I climbed into my personnel carrier, found my sleeping bag and snuggled down beneath the long bench that we sat on when we were in action.

Eventually I fell asleep, dreaming of being on a rifle range and turning my gun on my colleagues. I felt I was in control of what I was doing, deliberately choosing to kill them, wondering how many I could shoot before I was shot myself.

I was woken the next morning by voices outside the vehicle.

'Who nicked the bike?' someone was asking.

It took a few seconds for the full horror of what I'd done to come back to me.

I said nothing, trying to act as if it was just another day. I got up and washed. Someone made breakfast.

Before the exercise started, however, I owned up to taking the bike and was jovially instructed to take it back to where I'd found it. It looked like they were willing to put it down to nothing more than typical drunken high spirits.

I had no idea which house it had come from so I simply stacked it against the first one I came to, leaving as quickly as possible in case anyone spotted me.

'It's your turn to man the radio,' I was told when I got back.

My head was still throbbing from the night before and I didn't like the idea of having to concentrate on what people were saying. The person I had to listen and speak to was talking in my left ear while I monitored all the other communications with my right ear. If the people in my right ear required a reply, I had to switch a button to swap over. The pressure was building inside my head, but I battled on.

'Will all positions taking part in the exercise give their exact locations of yesterday evening,' a senior voice said in my right ear.

My stomach sank, my heart raced and my mouth dried. I knew my number was up.

An hour later a police car arrived and I was asked to get into it, escorted by one of the officers. I literally hung my head in shame as I was driven back to the village, which in the light of day looked as though a crime had never been committed there. I was taken to each of the places I'd visited on my drunken rampage and shown the damage I'd inflicted. How could I possibly explain why I'd wanted to attack the property of innocent people that I didn't even know? No one would ever be able to understand why I had done what I did because I didn't understand it myself. The rest of the day dragged by and I just wanted to get back to camp and hide away in my room. Eventually I was taken back there and I could tell from the looks that the gossiping had already started.

The next morning I dressed and paraded like everyone else, but in my heart I knew nothing would ever be the same again. The battery sergeant major confirmed, screaming at the top of his voice, that one of us had brought disgrace to the whole unit. I could tell everyone knew it was me and from now on my life was going to be hell. Not only did I have an Irish father, I had also brought the regiment's name into disrepute. I wanted to die, but the anger was still boiling inside me.

Just push me, I thought to myself, *any one of you fuckers from your lovely little lives. Push me and see what I can really do.*

That day, as punishment, I was given all the worst jobs to do and was escorted everywhere I went. I was even marched to and from the mess hall by a bombardier so that it was obvious to all the other batteries on the camp that I was a criminal of some sort. I had to speed-march on the spot and move forward only as and when he told me. I felt degraded and just wanted to leap at him and bite off his nose. He kept shouting his orders while I existed in two parallel worlds, one based in normality and one unspooling in my head like a movie. A part of me feared that at any moment I was going to do something I would regret for the rest of my life. I had to warn someone about what was going on inside my head.

'Permission to see the padre,' I said, towards the end of the afternoon.

The padre's room was simply furnished with just a desk and two chairs. There were a couple of religious plaques on the wall.

He was dressed in civilian clothes, a dog collar around his neck. I took a deep breath and started from the beginning, from the night my mother went to heaven. I told him of all the things I'd imagined doing to my fellow men since then, right up to the dream on the rifle range. He listened in silence, allowing me to get everything off my chest. I talked for over an hour.

'I'm glad you have come to me,' he said eventually. 'Don't worry any more. The Lord will watch over you and I will speak to the BSM about what you have told me.'

I went back to my room and waited until I was called back to the BSM's room. His attitude had changed completely. He spoke in a sympathetic voice, drained of all its parade ground ferocity.

'I'm taking you off guard duty rota,' he told me, 'and I'll speak to you again tomorrow morning.'

I was sent to Hanover hospital psychiatric ward, where the doctors dug a little deeper into my head. It was good to have someone paying me some attention, but at the same time I felt guilty about having given up the fight to hide and repress all my demons. Some of the guys from the unit came to visit me and I felt ashamed of being in hospital, as if I was admitting to a weakness.

After five or six weeks I was sent back to England.

Some money came through from *Private Eye*, £800 to start with and another £400 a few months later. It was as if the world was finally, grudgingly, admitting that we needed some help.

chapter thirteen

slipping into very bad ways

As I walked into the psychiatric ward of the Queen Elizabeth hospital in Woolwich, a man was sitting on the floor in front of the nurses' station with a pair of underpants on his head. Another patient told me he'd been serving as an officer in Northern Ireland and the stress had sent him off his head. Then a mixed-race youth told me he was pretending to be mad to get out of the Army. 'Come here,' he said, conspiratorially, 'I've got something to show you.'

I followed him to his bed space and he held his holdall open for me. I peered in and saw a handgun lying inside.

'Stole it before I was sent here,' he said, and I knew I needed to get out of there as quickly as possible.

The doctors went over everything with me again and I tried to make out that things were all right now that I was back in the UK.

'What do you want to do with your life?' one of them asked.

'I want to be back with my family,' I replied.

I was in regular contact with Debbie again and she came down to London to visit me with Sonia and Andy, who were now living together. They stayed at a local B&B and it cheered me up to see them.

The doctors agreed to let me go home to Leeds, as long as I returned for check-ups. I was moving from one day to the next, unsure what was going to happen; relieved to be out of the Army but confused as to how I felt about the future. The Army offered me a choice of resettlement courses to help me go back to Civvy Street. I chose driving and maintenance, knowing it would be a way to get my driving licence. I stayed with Debbie in her high-rise flat and in the end got another job at a direct sales company as a canvasser and appointment-maker, knocking on doors and talking home-owners into having a designer come round to their houses, pressuring them into buying new kitchens and bedrooms that they didn't really want or couldn't afford. I was good at it and they made me a team leader. I was proud to be doing well at something, but unhappy that I was involved with such a bad product.

Debbie and I were getting on well most of the time and decided to give it another shot. Then she became pregnant. Foolishly, we started talking about getting married, as couples do when they find themselves in that situation, but when she went for her three-month scan, we were told the baby had a severe case of spinabifida. We terminated the pregnancy.

It seemed I was continually lurching from one crisis to another. Not surprisingly, under such emotional pressure, things became very tense between us, but we stayed together. I liked being part of a steady couple.

When Debbie inherited £20,000 in her dad's will she packed in her job and started going to the casino every night and then on to nightclubs, living the high life. We quarrelled about it all the time because I thought the money offered her a real chance to make something of her life.

When Debbie told me she was lending a few hundred pounds to her cousin and a friend so they could go away on holiday I told her she'd never get it back. She wouldn't listen to me and I lost my temper, overturning the sofa and threatening to throw her out of the seventh-floor window. I sounded so aggressive that when I picked her up she genuinely thought I was going to do it. She fought and struggled and I kept the pretence going because I wanted her to think I was mad. Finally I let her go and grabbed the money, tearing it up and threatening to throw the pieces out the window. I knew, throughout this entire scene, that I was behaving just like the sort of men I hated the most.

In the end I calmed down, tidied up the flat and Sellotaped the money back together again, feeling ashamed and foolish. I went out with a friend that night and when I returned to the flat, Debbie's mum, who had obviously been told what had happened, burst out of the bedroom, screaming abuse and attacking me with a high-heeled shoe.

I moved in with Sonia, Andy and Leanne. Sonia and I would go out together a lot in the evenings and then she would go on to her blues clubs, leaving me to go home alone. I went with her a couple of times but found these dark, illegal parties frightening. Sonia just seemed to want to drink all the time, but I didn't really take any notice; she'd always been like that. Every weeknight she would regularly finish off four cans of lager. Things weren't good between her and Andy; they were arguing all the time.

Sonia would be in the pub most days, particularly the Vine, which had been one of Mum's old haunts. She could almost guarantee bumping into one of our many uncles in there, all of whom were heavy drinkers at the weekends after hard weeks on building sites. They would always look after her, buying her drinks and slipping her the odd £10 as they left to go to the next pub. They were family and they understood her, which not everyone did when she was drinking. She was running out of control. She told me that one morning she woke up at a massive house in Otley with no idea how she'd got there, or what had happened during the night.

In the early months of 1991 I got a job in the warehouse of a fashion wholesaler and applied to the council for a place of my own. It felt as if I might be getting somewhere at last and my confidence began to grow. The warehouse was close to Sonia's and so I would often go round at lunchtime to break up the day. On one of these occasions, when we were eating, there was a knock at the door, which, as the flat was above a shop, was on the ground floor. Sonia went down to see who it was.

'Someone for you,' she said, coming back up.

As I went downstairs I could see the door was ajar, revealing Debbie's uncle, a frightening looking man. He launched himself at me as I tried to scramble backwards up the stairs to safety. I could see another man standing in the shadows behind him, in case he needed help presumably. The blows kept raining down on me as I tried to protect myself and get back to the flat. Leanne was screaming and Sonia was shouting at the man to stop.

'This is for what you did to Debbie,' he snarled, then he turned on his heel and left, the front door still swinging open to the street.

Sonia and I concentrated on calming Leanne down and then I rang the police to tell them I'd been assaulted. They sent someone round but when the officer heard the whole story he suggested I would be wise to put it down to experience

The council came up with a flat for me, so at last I had a place of my own, although I had no furniture to speak of and no one to share it with. I was back to sleeping with any woman who was willing, sometimes more than one each weekend.

In December I was burgled and lost the few possessions I had. The following year my door was kicked in while I was at work and I was burgled again. I hated coming home now, always expecting to find the door broken open and all my things gone, and I was frightened of being in the flat alone.

After being broken into twice more I knew I had to get out of that place. My only option was to get a mortgage and try to climb onto the property ladder. It wasn't going to be easy since I had no capital and I was earning just £17,000 when I added in all my overtime but, with the help of a broker, I eventually managed to find a company that was willing to lend me what I needed. I began house-hunting in the green belt around Leeds. Going to look at these houses was like entering a different world, a world where people cared for their surroundings and worked to make their lives more pleasant. I found an old mid-terrace cottage with original open beams, a pine fitted kitchen, fitted bedroom furniture and a matching coloured bathroom, all luxuries that I'd never had before. As always with property transactions, there was going to be a delay, and I could hardly contain my impatience.

Andy and Sonia finally split and she stayed on in the flat with Leanne. I managed to talk my boss into giving her a job as my assistant, as I was implementing a computerised stock-control system for them, believing that I would be able to cover up for her if she'd been drinking. It worked for a while but then she started letting me down on Mondays, when she was recovering from her weekend binges, which never ended until she was too drunk to stand. Soon the problems spread to Tuesdays as well and it became obvious that she couldn't hold down the job. I had to tell her that it wasn't going to work.

Although I liked a drink myself I was very anti-drugs and smoking and couldn't understand why the lads at work were taking speed every weekend. I just couldn't see what all the fuss was about and told them so.

'Don't knock it till you've tried it,' one of them said. I was keen to prove to them that it was no big deal so I agreed. They gave me a small wrap of speed, which I swallowed, with a glass of water, as I was lying in the bath, getting myself ready to go out on a Saturday night. It was like a tiny bomb, wrapped in tissue, which would dissolve in my stomach, releasing the powder into my system.

I felt no effect at all as I finished dressing and set out for the town centre to meet a friend, Gary Rymer. It was a nice walk and every step that I took seemed more enjoyable than the last. As I strutted down the street, looking forward to the night ahead, it felt as if my whole body was sexually aroused. A smile spread across my face and as I caught sight of myself in the shop windows I was certain I was looking good. All my usual self-doubts had melted away and I knew it was due to the speed. It was the greatest feeling and now I regretted that I hadn't tried it sooner.

Gary felt the same as I did about drugs, so I didn't mention what I'd done, just chatted happily as we stood in the pub having a drink. My body kept moving to the music in the background, every muscle desperate to dance. I looked round at all the women, confident that every one of them fancied me. It felt very alien and very good. We went on to a nightclub and I danced on and on, feeling utterly wonderful, not even needing to have a drink. I could see Gary giving me strange looks; he could obviously tell that I wasn't myself.

When the end of the night came I still didn't feel ready to go home but there was nowhere else to go. By the time I reached my dismal flat all these feelings of elation had melted away, leaving only a deep, overwhelming sadness. I burst out sobbing as I struggled to stay in control of my emotions and not allow myself to be overcome by the misery. I felt desperate to talk to someone, to be near to another body, the loneliness inside me seeming like a bottomless pit. I couldn't bear to be alone for a second longer and drove to a friend's house, banging on the door until she let me in, spending the rest of the night lying beside her, crying and going over and over the past.

'How was it?' they asked when I went into work on Monday morning.

'OK,' I said, not wanting to admit how dire the comedown had been.

But they knew it had been more than OK when I asked for some more the next weekend, and every weekend after that. I couldn't wait to feel that high again, to be refilled with self-confidence and able to walk up to complete strangers and start conversations. Before long I was going out with the guys from work instead of Gary, discovering a whole new group of friends. With experience the comedowns became easier and the crying stopped. I had found a way to escape from myself.

The house purchase went through and I was able to move out of the flat and into an area where I could feel safe and clean at last. I wanted everything to be so pristine and well ordered, the complete opposite to the drabness, mess and squalor I'd grown up with. I decorated and furnished and made everything perfect. There was fresh cream paintwork and silver metallic blinds in the bathroom and bedroom, with matching metallic handles on the cupboards. Inside one of the fitted wardrobes was a large illuminated mirror with a shelf in front of it displaying neat rows of aftershave bottles, about thirty in all. I bought a large, tranquil picture of five grey pebbles on a cream background. Every time I walked into the house I felt my heart lift. I loved the feeling of order and cleanliness and everything being in its place. My shirts were neatly hung in order of colour, white followed by cream, green, blue, lilac and black. I ironed them with razor-sharp creases down the arms, making them crisp and ready to wear. I always wanted to be immaculately turned out, whether I was going to work or out on the town. I hated any stains or imperfections. I never wanted anyone to be able to say I wasn't perfectly clean and tidy. Just like when I was a child, I was always worrying about what other people thought of me, and tried to eliminate any fault in my appearance or my life. Every room in the house was tidy and carefully thought out. I was creating my own, perfect, controllable little world in the hope of feeling safe and secure at last.

Walking through Leeds one day soon after the move, I saw a man handing out fliers. I took one from him and glanced at it casually, poised to chuck it in the first bin I came to, when I saw Mum's face staring out at me. The flier was an advertisement for a book called *The Real Yorkshire Ripper*, claiming that Peter Sutcliffe was not the real Ripper, just a copycat killer. I stormed back to the man and asked who he was. He told me he was the author of the book and I started hurling abuse at him in the street, mustering all my self-control not to give in to the urge to hit him.

'Who are you?' he wanted to know. 'Why are you so upset?'

When I told him he became fascinated and gave me a copy of the book.

'Read it,' he urged me, 'and let me know what you think.'

At first the book scared me. What if there was some conspiracy that I knew nothing about? With Sonia I went over all the facts that the author put forward and we didn't know what to think. I contacted the police, who told me they'd heard of this man's theory and promised to send someone round to talk to me about it. Two CID officers came to try to reassure me and I didn't have the nerve to question anything they were saying. In the end it didn't matter to me who had actually killed Mum; the pain was still the same. Whenever I thought I'd started to put my childhood memories behind me, something would always turn up to relive them.

I was now out clubbing every weekend and the only bad effect was that I felt very ratty on Mondays and Tuesdays, my body aching from the weekend's abuse. With my new drug-induced confidence I'd chatted up a girl called Karen. She was in a different league from the sort of girls I usually went home with in my desperation for human contact. I was often high when I was chatting people up and so didn't always make the best judgements. Like so many of the girls I was attracted to when thinking clearly, on the other hand, Karen was smart and clean and bright and I thought once more that I had found the girl of my dreams.

When I wasn't on drugs I couldn't understand why a girl as normal as this would be interested in someone as abnormal as me. I became certain she would soon realise her mistake and dump me. She could tell that something was wrong and worked hard to get me to talk about the past and my anxieties. Bit by bit it all spilled out again. I was sure that now she was finding out more about me she would soon be gone and so I started sleeping with other women again whenever I wasn't with her, as if taking out an insurance policy against being dumped. But when

I was with her I wasn't able to keep the guilt from showing in my face and she knew something was up. When I confessed she didn't storm out, as I'd expected her to. She suggested instead that I should go and see a doctor.

I was referred to a clinical psychologist who saw me twice and told me my behaviour was quite normal and that he wished he'd slept around more when he was my age.

'Apparently my behaviour is normal,' I told Karen, but we both knew it wasn't and a few weeks later the relationship finally gave out under the strain, leaving me wrecked and heart-broken once more.

Since the doctor was no help I went to a homeopath that a friend had recommended. She thought I definitely did need help to curb my fears and control my jealous behaviour after listening to my story and I went to her house every couple of weeks for three months. She gave me some tablets as well, but any good these gentle cures might have done was washed away by the powerful chemicals I was swallowing every weekend.

Watching a police thriller about an investigation into the murder of a prostitute on television one evening, I found myself thinking once more about the investigation into Mum's death. A flashback to the murder on the television showed the woman being chased down a stairwell by a man, obviously distressed. I felt my heart rate rising. He caught her up and she was screaming as he stabbed her to death. I jerked up off the sofa as if I'd been given a massive electric shock.

'No!' I heard myself yelling. I felt as if Mum was being murdered in front of my eyes. And there was nothing I could do to save her. 'No, no, no!'

I sat, dazed, until the programme was over and a voice was reading out a help line number. I rang the number, not knowing what to expect. A woman answered and I explained what had happened and that I was alone and upset. She took my details and gave me two numbers, one for the Samaritans and another for an organisation called SAMM (Support After Murder and Manslaughter). Just talking to the woman at the Samaritans calmed me down and the people at SAMM started sending me details of their organisation and meetings I could attend. I never went to any of them but every few months I would receive a newsletter full of poems and short stories by parents, wives and friends of murder victims. I understood their pain. Mine felt as bad now as it had twenty years ago. I felt I needed the drugs to help me to forget. Having enjoyed the effects of speed so much, I had now discovered Ecstasy and with my new chemically induced self-confidence I'd taken to the clubbing scene like I'd been born to it. My clothes became more and more outrageous each week, screaming out for people to look at me, whether it was tartan kilts, bondage gear or satin suits. I was buying my E's from a friend, who pointed out that it would be a lot cheaper and safer if I was to buy them from him before going out for the night rather than paying over the odds to strangers in clubs. It made sense and I started by asking him for four E's for a small group of us each week. Before long I was buying them for all the people I was going to the clubs with, paying £7 each and selling them for £10. To begin with that just meant about a dozen people, but the numbers started to rise as friends of friends asked me to buy for them. The profit I made each week from the tablets meant that my nights out normally ended up costing me nothing. Without making any conscious decision to do so, I'd become a small-time dealer.

I was becoming known as a character in the club we frequented the most, befriending the bouncers, using a bit of banter to get past them without being searched. When a dance music magazine sent a photographer one weekend he immediately picked me out as I showed off on the dance floor in a kilt and matching tartan top hat, and the picture appeared in an article about the club. On another occasion, a film crew turned up on a night when I was flaunting a yellow tartan suit, which I'd got a tailor to run up for me from material I'd chosen myself. Out of my mind on E's, I had no idea what was going on, at one point striding up to the bar and ordering a drink without realising I was standing next to the presenter of the programme.

When the film was shown I found people coming up to me in the street, recognising me as the guy in the tartan suit. A friend's father was a presenter on *The Money Programme* and he asked if we would appear in a documentary about 'Generation X'. The television crew came to my house on a Saturday and spent the whole day filming us. We watched videos of adverts and were asked for our opinions. None of us had had any sleep the night before, having been out in the clubs, and weren't thinking very straight. One of the side effects of drugs is forgetting what you're saying halfway through sentences. They kept asking us to repeat things for the cameras, but we couldn't remember what we'd just said. It seemed funny at the time, although I doubt if the film crew were as amused as we were. At ten o'clock we told them we were going out and they filmed us getting ready, following us to the club and filming us dancing. By then it was obvious we were part of the drugs scene. When it was shown a few weeks later everyone rang to say they'd seen us. People came up to me in the clubs and on the street and I felt like I'd become a star.

chapter fourteen

stitched up

The nightlife in Leeds is good. Sometimes, on a warm summer evening, it can feel more like a coastal resort than a landlocked northern city. The streets are full of people in high spirits, enjoying the benefits of alcohol and illegal substances, not worrying about their downsides. Groups of people drift across the roads with no thought for the traffic, the women in their low-cut tops and short skirts showing off cleavages and tanned legs, enticing boisterous young men to shout suggestive remarks and banter loudly with one another. People sing as they weave from pub to pub, flirting and laughing. I love my home town when it is like that.

I was dating three women at the beginning of 1995, one of whom was a sweet girl called Louise. When I realised I was falling for her I gave up the other two and started seeing her most nights. We would go clubbing together and some nights we would stop at my house, sometimes hers. Her parents were great and treated me just like a son, but after a few months I started going out without her and sleeping with other girls, just as I had before. As with Karen, I wasn't able to hide my betrayals from her, which would make her cry and then forgive me, over and over again. I knew I was treating her badly, but the drugs and my desperate need to be liked was too powerful a cocktail to resist. I hated myself for my own weakness and often told her I wanted to end the relationship because I couldn't stop myself from sleeping around. She stuck by me.

It was only a matter of time before I would make a mistake and get myself into serious trouble, but I was so out of it most of the time I never saw the direction it was coming from. I had a friend called Ray, who used to buy pills from me at weekends and would come round to the house now and then for a smoke. His boss had been in prison for dealing drugs and there was a rumour on the streets that he was now an informer. Some of us confronted Ray with this but he dismissed our fears as ridiculous. I remember one night when he split up with his girlfriend and came round to my house in a terrible state, looking for a shoulder to cry on. I was always very sympathetic to anyone who was hurting from a broken relationship, having been there so many times myself.

My lifestyle was beginning to affect my work. After phoning in sick and taking two weeks off I found myself included in a redundancy programme. I received a pay-off of a couple of thousand pounds and decided to combine business with pleasure and go into promoting dance nights.

I hired a local club for the night and called it 'Fever', running a talent showcase for up-and-coming DJs. I asked them to send in tapes and if they were any good I agreed to let them play for an hour each. I had posters and fliers printed and stuck them up in all the trendy shops. I contacted a local magazine and they sent someone down to do a write-up on the night. It went well and the club asked me to run another night on a Thursday. I tried other venues as well, but always on weekdays because the weekends were run by the established promoters. Then I heard a rumour that a club owner was suffering from a drop in attendance on Friday nights, so I went to see him, clutching a bunch of fliers for other events I'd organised. He said he was willing to give me a go. I finally had a weekend club night. It was a bit like a family night out, as all my sisters and their boyfriends and Louise came. I used some of the DJs from my talent night as well as some of the more established ones. I hired vocalists and sometimes even limousines to be given away to lucky clubbers. But it was an up-and-down business. I usually made no profit, although my weekends out paid for themselves.

However much I might have been enjoying myself, I eventually had to admit that I wasn't making a living in the promoting game. I had to get a proper job if I wasn't going to fall behind with the mortgage and lose my beloved house. I went to work in the despatch department of another fashion wholesaler and got some routine back into my life. I was still buying E's for friends in order to fund my clubbing, and Sonia was taking drugs regularly at weekends too, when Leanne would stay with Andy's parents. It was heartbreaking to see her losing her grip on being a good mother when her daughter meant so much to her, but there was no doubt Leanne was much better off spending time in the steady life of her grandparents.

Then, every Tuesday and Wednesday night I started to have out-of-body experiences whenever I shut my eyes, my head spinning as I dreamed I was leaving the bed and rising above the house. I actually started to enjoy the sensation and believed I could control it to some degree. Sometimes I would start falling back down to the bed at great speed, trying to scream with no sound coming out of my mouth and having to be woken by Louise, shaking and sweating. I knew it was a build-up of the drugs I'd taken at the weekend, but I was enjoying myself too much to think about stopping. As I poured the drugs into my system in an attempt to escape the reality of my life, I ignored the potential dangers, thinking they would never affect me.

After one particularly heavy weekend, I didn't have the strength to get up on the Monday. I was going to have to ring in sick, but when I tried my voice out I couldn't think what I was trying to say. It was like a nightmare. I'd lost the power of speech. Words started to spill out in no particular order. I picked up the phone anyway and after a few wrong numbers managed to get through to my supervisor, mumbling that I wouldn't be in. I could hear he was talking to me but I couldn't make sense of the words. I tried out a few possible replies. The moment I hung up I collapsed on the floor, the effort of trying to make conversation too much.

I finally managed to get into work on Tuesday and kept my head down. I knew I was going to have to get my life together. I stayed off drugs for a few weeks, although I was still getting them for Ray, which was a nuisance, but I didn't know how to say no to him.

Walking through Leeds one evening, I saw a woman being helped into a taxi by what looked like her friends. She was so drunk she could barely walk, her legs dragging along the ground like a wounded soldier being rescued from the battlefield by colleagues. She was shouting obscenities at everyone around her and as I drew closer I realised it was Sonia, my beautiful sister.

'Sonia?' I tried to speak to her but she didn't seem to register that it was me.

'Don't worry,' her friends assured me, 'we'll stay with her.'

As I stood in the street, helplessly watching the taxi drawing away, I started to cry. How could she have got into such a state? How could we both have ended up so desperate, when we cared for each other so much?

As I came home from work one evening in July, a car I didn't recognise drew up outside the house. Ray was in the passenger seat and an older man was behind the wheel. They got out.

'What do you want?' I asked Ray.

'This is my friend,' Ray said, introducing the confident, rugged man with him. There was something threatening about him, even though he was being friendly. 'He's been let down by someone and needs to buy a hundred E's.'

My stomach gave a lurch of foreboding. My instincts told me I was being set up, and I remembered the rumours I'd heard about Ray's boss.

'I don't want to get involved in anything like this,' I told them.

'Oh, don't worry,' his boss said, brushing aside my protests, 'it won't be for a few weeks. We'll get in touch.'

I felt a wave of relief as they left, hoping they'd got the message that I didn't want anything to do with them, but a few weeks later Ray rang in the middle of the week saying he wanted the pills the following evening. Not wanting to upset anyone, particularly Ray's dangerous looking boss, but still not wanting to get involved, I asked the person I usually bought from if I could pass his details on.

'No.' He was adamant. 'I can't trust anyone I don't know, but I can still handle the business. I'll meet you with the E's in a few hours.'

I should have said no and put a stop to the whole thing then and there, but I didn't, even though my stomach was on spin cycle as I drove to the meeting place. Every car I saw looked as if the occupants were plain-clothes police. I picked up the pills as normal and drove home, telling myself that I was worrying about nothing, that I would do this one deal and then tell them I didn't want to do it again. I didn't want to have the pills at home so I stopped on an empty road outside the village, lifting the bonnet of the car as if I had a mechanical problem. Reaching through a hole in the hedge I scraped away some soil and hid the bag, making a mental note of where it was.

Ray was back on the phone the moment I got in from work the next day.

'The guy who wants them is ready to take delivery,' he told me. 'We'll meet you at the coach station in Leeds now.'

He wouldn't even give me time to get something to eat. I had to go to the meeting straight away. I went back out, pulling the front door behind me, and climbed into the car. There was someone standing beside the phone booth about forty yards from the house. Was he watching me? My heart was thumping. I drove away from the house and saw the man secrete something in his jacket, get into his car and leave. A little way down the road I turned and went back. The nervous tension was making me feel nauseous. I got out of the car and watched the man driving away from the village. It just didn't seem right and I sat for a few moments, wondering what to do. Since I didn't have any incriminating evidence in the car I thought I could get away with driving around for a while. I got back into the car and headed out to the road where the pills were hidden. Within a mile I passed the mysterious man once again. When I got to the place where I'd hidden the bag I stopped the car. There was no sign of anyone else so I scooped the tablets up from under the hedge and pushed them down into the crotch of my pants.

With my heart pounding so hard I could hardly breathe, I headed for the coach station in the city centre. Every other driver on the road seemed to be deliberately trying to infuriate me, either going ridiculously slowly or recklessly fast. I wanted to get rid of the pills as quickly as possible. I planned to put them in a locker at the station so that I wouldn't actually be handing them over. The journey seemed to be taking for ever and I spotted an empty bus lane, pulling into it in the hope of speeding up my journey. A blue light was immediately flashing in my mirror.

Shit, I thought. Stay cool. Don't make them suspicious.

I pulled the car to the side. Stay calm, stay calm. They may just have seen the bus lane offence. The police car pulled up behind me and the driver sat in the car while his colleague climbed out with agonising slowness and walked towards me.

I wound down the window and tried to smile. 'Sorry,' I said when he reached me. 'I shouldn't have gone into that lane.'

'Would you step out of your car, please, sir, and follow me to my car.'

I obeyed, aware that I was close to losing my nerve. They asked my name and ran a check on me as I sat in the car with them.

'Where are you going?' they asked while they waited for the results.

'To my sister's.'

'I'm going to search your car, sir,' the first policeman told me. 'Am I likely to find anything?'

'Nothing at all,' I said, quite truthfully.

I watched as he went through the car methodically, horribly aware of the uncomfortable package in my pants. I tried to control my facial expressions so they didn't give any signs of guilt.

After what seemed like an age he strolled back to the police car and climbed back in.

'OK,' he said. 'I believe you may be carrying some form of illegal substance, so I'm going to search you.'

I knew now the game was up.

I climbed out of the car. I now had nothing to lose and my nerve cracked. In a blind panic I made a dash for it. I don't think my heart can have been in it and my legs felt like lead. He grappled me to the ground before I'd got more than a few yards, cutting his hand as we fell to the floor. The driver jumped out to come to his assistance as the rush-hour traffic continued to flash past. The pills had fallen out of their hiding place in the scuffle. The second policemen picked them up.

'I suppose these are yours?' he said.

They read me my rights, handcuffed me and guided me back into the car. In the station I was booked, fingerprinted, photographed and locked in a cell. Suddenly I was alone and I wished I was dead. I lay down on the plastic-covered mattress and thought of everything I was now likely to lose: my job, my house and probably Louise once she found out what had happened. I would slip back down to the bottom of the pile, all the progress I had managed to make wiped away overnight. I was sure I'd been set up, but that didn't change the fact that I was a dealer, even if only in a small way, and that I had been really stupid. I tried holding my breath, like I used to do as a child, in the vain hope that I could suffocate myself and escape all the humiliations that now lay in store.

The police, hoping they'd got someone bigger than they had, went to my house to search for more drugs, coming away empty-handed. They brought my Filofax back to the station and interrogated me on every name and address. I told them the drugs weren't mine, that I'd been ordered to deliver them to someone at the bus station. I wanted to tell them I knew they'd set me up and the whole process was a charade, but I didn't have the nerve. They wanted the name and number of my supplier, but I told them I couldn't give them anything since I didn't know anything about him.

'We just meet in a pub once a week,' I said, 'and this week he told me to deliver these pills for him and he would give me some for the favour.'

'You're looking at a long prison sentence here,' they warned me. 'But if you agree to help us out in the future we could get you bail and you won't have to go on remand straight away. But if you let us down,' they warned, 'we'll come and lift you.'

We talked on and on and in the end they agreed to let me go if I promised to call them in a few weeks with a name and a number. Since I just wanted to get out of that station and back to my house, I agreed. I went home and went to bed, knowing that my whole life was about to cave in. When I woke up in the morning I was determined to enjoy every day of freedom that was left to me. I told Louise what had happened and she cried.

'I told you to stop the pills,' she said.

I knew she was right.

Sonia cried too.

I told my supplier and he said not to worry about paying him and thanked me for warning him. I rang Ray and told him I wanted to meet. He seemed surprised to hear from me and we made an arrangement for lunchtime. I told him what had happened.

He said nothing, then promised to help me with the name of a good solicitor. I noticed the telltale signs of a white substance forming at the corners of his mouth. I knew that even if I'd made it to the coach station there would have been no one there to meet me. I hated him.

I found a solicitor of my own, telling him the same story as I had the police, that I'd been forced into it. At work I told them I'd bumped into a bus in the bus lane and was being charged with reckless driving.

The legal process started slowly, with a run of small hearings at the magistrates' court and I had to contact the probation service to get them to write a report. Louise was there on the day the probation officer came round to the house. He told us there was a chance I wouldn't be sent to prison as, in his opinion, nothing would be gained from it. I had my own home, a job and no criminal record to speak of. He was very sympathetic and told me not to worry.

A few weeks later the police rang again and asked if I would work with them, picking people out in nightclubs for them to arrest, but these clubbers were all my friends and there was no way I would be able to grass on them.

'I'm not a drug dealer,' I said, 'so I can't help you.'

The officer wished me luck before putting the phone down.

I stopped going clubbing, getting a job behind the bar in a dance music club instead in order to earn some extra cash and still be able to be out in the atmosphere that I loved. Most of the people there were on drugs and one night Ray came up to the bar.

'How are you?' he asked.

'As well as can be expected.'

'Don't worry,' he said. 'I've been talking to a copper friend of mine and he thinks you'll get off, not having been in trouble before.'

He kept coming to the club over the next few weeks. Just after midnight one night all the lights suddenly went on, the music died and the club was crawling with fifty or more police officers, menacing in black combat clothing. Various people who must have been pointed out to them were dragged outside and dogs were brought in to sniff everyone else. I had to clear up the bar and was the last to leave, with the manager and a friend who was working as cloakroom girl. The clubbers had all dispersed but there were still plenty of police outside, including a cameraman who had filmed the proceedings. I saw Ray chatting to some high-ranking officers. I went over.

'What are you doing here?' I asked.

He quickly ushered me to one side. 'Keep the noise down, mate,' he said, 'I've got drugs in the car. I was just trying to bullshit my way out of the situation.'

Now I knew for sure that he was the police spotter who had identified all the dealers that evening, having bought drugs off them earlier.

I found I couldn't get him out of my mind and when he turned up at the club again a few weeks later I followed him to the toilet. I started shouting at him, accusing him of setting me up while he kept denying it. He left the toilet, and as I went back to the bar a few minutes later I heard him on the payphone, repeating our conversation to someone. Still boiling with anger, I stood over him, glaring into his face. I'd never been a fighter but I was so angry with this guy, who I had thought was a friend, for potentially depriving me of my freedom. He ended his call and went back to the dance floor, studiously avoiding the bar for the rest of the night.

One day the following week I got home from work and made myself some dinner as usual. Taking it through from the kitchen to the living room I saw Ray and his boss glaring in at me through the glass of the front door.

The older man started banging on the door. 'Open this door!' he shouted.

Forcing myself to stay calm, I put the tray down on the coffee table and opened the door. The moment I did, Ray's boss went for my throat, pushing me hard into a corner of the living room that no one could see from outside.

'Stop spreading your fucking rumours,' he snarled, his face just inches from mine, 'or next time I'll be round with a shotgun and I'll blow your kneecaps away.'

Ray stood looking over his boss's shoulder. How different he'd been a few months before when he'd come to my house and poured out all his girlfriend troubles.

Louise was having problems handling the pressure of her parents finding out I was a dealer and we decided to call the relationship off. I couldn't blame her. Life with me was becoming pretty bleak, with the likelihood of it getting worse.

I was committed to crown court for sentencing on 2 January 1997. I'd met a girl called Jenny by that time. She was beautiful, blonde, slim and sexy, and she didn't care about the drugs charge. She worked for a local newspaper and did some part-time modelling. I was gobsmacked when she invited me to her parents' house. It was in the middle of nowhere with a kitchen the size of my entire house. I felt totally out of my depth. Her mother asked if I would like a drink; I asked for a cup of tea and knew I was in a different world when the silverware came out.

I later discovered that her mother told her not to 'lower herself', that she should look for someone who would be able to support her so she wouldn't have to work. 'I don't want my grandchildren to grow up wearing shell suits,' she said.

All through Christmas I became increasingly nervous. Jenny came to my house a lot and, encouraged by my probation officer's assurance that they would take my childhood circumstances into consideration, we told each other that I would probably just have to pay off a fine and do a few hundred hours community service. Then we would be able to put the whole thing behind us. Deep in my heart I wasn't so confident.

chapter fifteen
prison life

Dad was always trying to persuade Pauline to take him back and from time to time she would weaken and agree. On one of these occasions she fell pregnant and gave birth to Kirsty, my youngest sister. But it wasn't long before the demon drink raised its head again and Pauline went back to bringing up her children on her own. She was a good woman and her great misfortune was to fall in love with Dad when she was too young to know better. Over the years he gradually forced her to fall out of love with him, and then left her to bring up her children with no financial support at all. It was a job she never shirked, any more than she shirked the task of taking on me and my sisters when we were presented to her. She once promised Angela that she would never leave us until we were grown up, and she stuck to her word as best she could, despite the many beatings.

Although lots of people, including my probation officer, had told me they thought I would be let off with a slap on the wrist and some community service, I was growing increasingly nervous as my day in court drew closer. What if they were all wrong? What if I ended up going to prison and became a convicted drug dealer? What future would I have then?

New Year's Day hung around our necks like a death sentence. Jenny and I tidied the house, as if preparing to go away on holiday, and all the time I kept thinking about how I would be unable to keep up my mortgage repayments if I was sent to prison, which would mean they would take the house away and I would be back where I started at the bottom of the heap. My heart felt more and more like lead as every hour passed and the day of reckoning drew closer. I ironed my clothes in preparation for the hearing the next day, trying to give myself the illusion of being in control, if only of my own appearance. I'd decided to wear a green woollen jacket and black trousers, wanting to look smart and respectful of the judge, but not like a prosperous drug dealer. We went to bed early; what else was there to do?

The next morning Jenny drove us to court. We passed through the metal detectors at the courthouse and found a noticeboard that told us what court I would be appearing in and the name of the judge who would decide my future. I wished I had known if he had a reputation for being lenient or not. There was a little while to wait so we went up to the canteen for a cup of tea. There was no way I could have eaten anything. To my amazement Dad walked in with Sonia and her current boyfriend, a dark-haired, muscular bricklayer called Neil, whom I knew fairly well by this point, but whose jealousy and possessiveness as far as Sonia was concerned had always worried me. I was touched to see Dad there, but too distracted by my worries really to take anything in.

As we sat, talking quietly, looking around at everyone else and trying to imagine what they were there for, my solicitor arrived and told me to come with him to meet the barrister who was going to present my mitigating circumstances to the judge and discuss with him, behind closed doors, the charge and my plea. I was pleading guilty to possession of a controlled substance with the intent to supply. I was taken to a desk in a cubicle where the barrister was waiting. He shook my hand and said he was pleased to meet me.

'I've read your case notes,' he said once I'd sat down, 'and your probation report. In my opinion you shouldn't even be here. It's a cruel world.'

I wasn't sure if he meant I shouldn't be there because of what had happened to Mum, or whether he believed I had been forced into carrying the drugs. I said nothing, but I felt a small flicker of hope.

'What do you think will happen to you?' he asked.

'I don't know,' I admitted. 'My probation officer told me he didn't think there would be any point in them sending me to prison.'

He shook his head sadly. 'I'm sorry to be the one to break this to you, but there is no way you will be going home today. I'm afraid you've been led down the garden path there.'

The shock passed through my body in a wave as I struggled to understand the full meaning of his words. It felt as if all my blood had drained away, leaving me feeling limp and dazed. I was going to prison, away from Jenny, Sonia, my friends, my house and my freedom. I jumped out of my seat, gasping for breath, as if I'd been punched in the stomach, running my fingers frantically through my hair.

'No! No!' I shouted. 'I have a house. I'll lose my house. I won't have a job. My life won't be worth living.'

'Calm down, Richard,' he said.

I sat with my head in my hands for several minutes. 'What am I looking at?' I asked, when I could get my thoughts together enough to take in any information he could give me.

'Two to three years, I should think,' he said, and I felt the tears coming to my eyes. 'Say goodbye to everyone before we have to go in.'

As I walked back into the canteen like a zombie I was aware of Dad and the others all looking up and smiling at me encouragingly. As I drew closer, they saw my face and their expressions changed.

'I'm going down,' I said. 'I may get three years.' I went to Jenny and kissed her. 'I love you,' I told her. 'Please wait for me.'

Then the solicitor came back in and told me not to take too much money with me. I had £60 in my pocket so I kept a fiver and gave the rest to Sonia.

'Richard,' Neil said urgently, 'before you go, come to the toilets with me.'

I followed him, too shocked to be able to think for myself.

As soon as we were in the toilets he pulled a big block of cannabis resin out of his pocket and rolled it into a ball.

'Take this in with you,' he said. 'It'll be currency on the prison wings.'

I watched in horror as he tore up the bag it was in and made a Cellophane ball out of it. He then took out his lighter and started to seal it with the flame.

'You're gonna have to shove it up your bum,' he explained, 'and then you'll be OK once you're inside.'

'Richard!' my solicitor burst in. 'Come on, you're being called.'

I went straight out to the courtroom, leaving Neil and his drugs behind. I was feeling ill with anxiety as I was guided to stand behind a high glass screen. As I looked out into the room I saw Jenny and Sonia and the others walking in and sitting down in a line of seats along the wall. The usher announced the judge and we rose. When the judge sat down, we all did the same. The judge talked and my barrister talked and their words washed over me; all I could think about was going to prison. The judge said he understood that I had apparently been forced to carry the drugs but that he had no choice other than to give me a custodial sentence.

I think I was asked to stand at this point and I know I was crying. I couldn't bring myself to look over at my family. I just stared directly in front of me and waited for the blow to fall.

'I sentence you to twelve months imprisonment.'

Despite the confirmation that I was going to prison, I knew I'd got off lightly. The judge had decided to give me a break because of Mum.

'If you ever appear before me again,' he warned, 'you must expect to receive the maximum penalty.'

A door opened behind me and a security officer took hold of my arm, guiding me out. I had to stop crying now and face up to whatever lay in store. I was walked to some sort of desk where my details were given, forms filled in and my sentence registered before being taken to a small cell. A few minutes later my solicitor came to tell me that the room where relatives could say their goodbyes was out of order, so I wouldn't be able to see them before I was taken away.

'It's OK,' I told him, suddenly aware that I was not going to get what I wanted from now on.

I sat on my own in the cell for a couple of hours. Someone brought me a sandwich and I could hear a group of lads shouting to one another in the next cell. They were talking about friends who'd been arrested for some Post Office robbery and speculated about what sentence they were likely to get. I felt the familiar sensation of being an outsider trapped in an alien and threatening world.

Around dinnertime the door opened and I was led into a corridor where the others from the cells were already standing. We were escorted into a yard with high walls where a white Group 4 security van was waiting for us with its small black windows. We climbed in through a low door in the back, each of us placed into one of the tight cubicles that lined both sides. The seat was hard. Although no one could see in through the windows, we could see out. Once everyone was seated the door was locked behind us and the van headed for HMP Armley. I craned round to look out of the window, desperately hoping to catch a glimpse of Sonia or Jenny but they weren't there. They had returned to their lives hours ago and I was on my own now.

At first sight, Armley looked like a gloomy black castle on a hill. Although things were supposed to be changing there, it had a reputation for bullying and suicides amongst inmates. As we walked into reception, they took our names, photographed us, and I became prisoner DN1454. I told them I hadn't thought I would be coming to jail and they laughed. One kind officer asked if I wanted to make a call. I jumped at the chance of hearing a friendly and familiar voice and rang Pauline's number. Jenny and Sonia were both there.

They told me that once my solicitor had told them I was OK, Dad left and the rest of them went off to the pub where they drank whisky together and couldn't think of anything to say.

'It was like someone had died,' Sonia told me.

When I got back to the cell everyone was asking each other what they were in for. When I told them I'd got twelve months for dealing I could see they were all surprised by the leniency of the sentence. I wanted to tell them about Mum, in case they thought I was a grass, but it didn't seem the right moment to start spilling out my whole life story.

We handed in our clothes and were given prison uniforms of denim trousers, red T-shirts and cheap socks and shoes. We were sent to the shower area to change and a guy asked if I had any foil. I told him no and he went straight to the next guy. He eventually got some and started smoking his bit of crack or whatever it is you need foil for. I was determined to keep myself clear of the whole drugs scene in prison. After a spell in a holding cell, with more prisoners joining us, we were escorted to A Wing and I was put into a cell with a guy who'd been given four weeks for driving while banned. We exchanged a few words but I didn't feel like talking. I had the lower bunk and there was a small toilet beside it, but no privacy. The walls were bare and the big black door had a little glass circle in it, which the officers peered through at regular intervals.

We lay on our bunks, doing nothing for a few hours, until we were asked to leave our cell to fetch our evening meals, which were served through a hatch by other prisoners. It was some sort of pasta with mince and a bowl of rice pudding and a plastic mug of tea, which we ate in our cells. I was surprised to find myself enjoying it, but I guess I hadn't eaten much since the previous day. It didn't seem that different to being on an exercise in the Army and I began to think I would be able to make it through the ordeal if I just kept focused on one day at a time.

By nine that night I wanted to get to sleep as quickly as possible, eager to finish the first day of my sentence, but the shouts of other prisoners on the three-storey wing made it impossible. There was a constant stream of abuse flying around, and messages being yelled from cell to cell, keeping me awake for hours. There was also a procedure where someone would tie a package to a piece of string and drop it out of their window, swinging it to the next cell. That person would do the same and the package would make its way slowly to its destination, one window at a time. No one ever stole a passing package because everyone would have been able to tell who the culprit was. All the other prisoners seemed to know who everyone else was, but I knew no one. I was just an anonymous number, and that was how I wanted to stay. I didn't want to do anything to draw attention to myself. I wanted to be as small and invisible as possible. I eventually got to sleep in the small hours, only to be jerked awake again by the bang of keys on the door at seven-thirty.

We got dressed and went for breakfast. At ten o'clock the new arrivals were gathered together in a room. I was the only one who hadn't been in prison before. An officer explained that we would be given the opportunity to learn new skills and to have jobs that would earn us a small wage. He showed us a video about bullying and suicide in prison and asked us to look out for other people if they seemed at all down. Then I was taken to see the doctor.

'Will you be getting any script?' another inmate asked as we waited our turn.

'No,' I said, knowing he meant medication.

'Tell them you're on heroin, then they'll give you a dose of methadone each day, and they'll give you tablets you can use as currency.'

I ignored the advice and told the doctor I was fine.

We were allowed to mix together in the afternoon outside the cells but I didn't know who to talk to so I sat in front of the television and stared at a film, trying to look as if I wasn't bothered about being there on my own. There was a bookshelf on the wing and when the film finished I spent some time browsing through the books. I picked up one about Edward and Mrs Simpson, thinking that reading would be a good way to pass some of the time and would give me something else to do with my hands and eyes. I was keen not to make eye contact with anyone until I was more confident of who was who. I'd never really read books before and I was surprised how quickly I got into it, escaping from the thoughts and worries that were buzzing around my head. I'd finished it by the next morning.

During the coming months I discovered the works of John Grisham and Gerald Seymour. I loved the way good always triumphed in Grisham's books and Seymour took me to worlds I knew little about like the Middle East and Ireland.

Armley is normally a holding prison where prisoners are either on remand or waiting to be shipped somewhere else. The following day I was told I was going to be sent to some distant Category C prison. I had no idea where it was but it sounded a long way from Leeds and all my friends and family. I pleaded with the prison officer, explaining that we were a close family but that no one had a car.

'Wait there,' she said eventually, 'I'll see what I can do.'

She made a phone call and then told me not to worry, that she'd got me a job in the hospital wing and that I wasn't going to be shipped off anywhere. I didn't tell anyone else in case it pissed them off, but I knew I'd been lucky.

The hospital wing consisted of four corridors, arranged in a square. At the northern end there was a day room with TV, video, pool table, comfortable chairs, books and a computer. Beside it was an officers' station and then through another gate was the place that I was now going to be calling home, which included a small kitchen, a shower area and six beds with lockers between them. It was like being back in the Army. At the far end of the room was a TV, which could be seen from all the beds. As a newcomer I would start in the bed furthest from the screen and then, as other inmates left, I would move up.

My new cellmates seemed decent guys. The most senior, the one nearest the TV, was called John. He'd been given four years for smuggling drugs into the country in his truck, although he said he knew nothing about it. Paddy had also received four years for knowingly or unknowingly giving information that led to a wages snatch at the company he worked for. Tommy, a mean-looking guy, was close to finishing a two-year sentence for dealing. Then there was Frank, who I'd already met and who'd told me the hospital wing was a cushy number, and Leslie, a stocky ex-financial adviser, who was in for a fraud. He too claimed he was innocent. Everyone, it seemed, was innocent except me.

My job was to brush and mop all the corridors in the doctors' areas every day, and to hoover, clean and empty the wastepaper baskets in their offices. I was also on call to make cups of tea and coffee for anyone who asked, including the governor. I always felt privileged when I entered his office. I was paid £2.70 for my week's work and I gave good value, keeping those corridors spotless and making drinks with as much care as if I was running my own little restaurant. I also helped with the distribution of meals from the kitchens. Even with all my duties, I still managed to find a lot of time to read.

Letters were like a lifeline to the outside world, especially Sonia's, which were so funny. She'd contacted everyone I owed money to like the mortgage company, the bank, and the credit card, utilities and telephone companies to explain what had happened. She even went to the Citizens Advice Bureau to ask what else we should be doing. She was looking after her little brother again, just as she'd done when we were tiny. She begged Donna and Angela to write to me as well to keep my spirits up, but they weren't really interested. Who could blame them? They had enough problems in their own lives without taking responsibility for me. I dare say they thought I'd brought my troubles on myself.

Leslie helped me with the wording of the letters I had to send. 'Offer to pay the mortgage company something every month,' he advised, 'even if it's only ten pounds.'

Sonia did that for me and made the payments, even though she was on benefits. She also found money to send into prison for me. Even Dad managed to contribute £40. I also received a couple of short letters from him, which really pleased me. I could imagine how much of an effort writing them must have been and I appreciated it more than I would ever be able to tell him.

When I was given my letters from Jenny I'd take them down to the doctor's surgery and read them over and over again. She would dab her perfume onto the paper so that I could hold them to my nose, fill my head with her smell and think of her. After two weeks I was told I could send out a visiting order and I sent it out with Jenny and Sonia's names on. I couldn't wait to see them. I was allowed one visit a month, and if I behaved, that would go up to two a month. Soon I would be able to see Jenny every fortnight.

'If you look out the window,' the other lads explained to me on that first visiting day, 'you can see the visitors' car park over the wall.' One of them gave me a red plastic sheet about the size of a flag with the words 'I love you' in large white letters. By closing one corner of the sheet in the window, and the other in the next window, I could hang the message up for my visitors to see. I desperately tried to spot Jenny's car, but I couldn't.

Anyone expecting a visit was rounded up and taken to a room with about thirty chairs around the walls. I didn't catch anyone's eye, just stared at the graffiti and tried not to breathe in too much of the smoke from the cigarettes everyone else seemed to be smoking.

The door opened, a few names were read out and the prisoners who'd been called stood up and walked out. The process was repeated a few minutes later but my name still didn't come up. It felt like waiting at Beckett's Park for Dad to turn up. On the third time they called for McCann and I was given a red bib to wear over my clothes as I walked down a long room through two lines of tables and sat at the one they pointed out to me. Other prisoners were already sitting at the tables and some of the visitors were crying and hugging them. A gate opened to my left and Jenny and Sonia walked through. Jenny was by far the most beautiful person in the room and looked very out of place. I saw other prisoners glancing up at her as she walked towards me. The fact that she turned heads wherever she went made me proud but troubled me. I'm sure a more secure man wouldn't have had a problem with it, but I was always expecting to be hurt and dumped.

Sonia got there first and I stood to hug her. I could smell Jenny's perfume long before she reached me. As I hugged and kissed her I forced myself not to let the tears come into my eyes. We all sat down and I held Jenny's hand tightly. I only had an hour with them and I was terrified that it was already slipping away at a terrible rate. Jenny told me she was moving out of her parents' house and was planning to get a place of her own. I begged her to move into my house so that everything would be OK with the mortgage company and so I would know where she was. She wouldn't agree and I was starting to become upset. But I'd only been going out with her a few months and was putting too much pressure on her.

'Calm down, Richard,' Sonia urged. 'Everything will be OK.' I couldn't stop kissing Jenny and eventually Sonia said she would go to the waiting room to give us some privacy. Kissing her was making me feel alive, the best feeling I'd had for weeks.

All too soon time was up. 'Before you go, drive into the car park and look up at the windows,' I said finally, as we were parted.

I felt full of pride as she walked out amongst the other visitors, looking like a princess. I ran to our room and looked out of the window next to my sign. Only one car remained in the car park and it was Jenny's. She was standing at the driver's door with Sonia on the other side and they were both waving. I waved back and wanted to keep waving for ever to stop them from leaving. I was unable to stop tears from coming. Eventually they climbed back into the car and I watched as it drove away, tearing my heart out with it.

I went to join the others in the kitchen. I could still smell Jenny on my hands as I ate my food. When we finished I didn't want to wash the plates in the sink because I knew I would wash away her perfume, but I didn't have the nerve to ask one of the others to wash my plates for me just so I could continue to sniff my girlfriend on my skin.

Valentine's Day was approaching and I bought Jenny a card out of my wages and asked Sonia to put a message in the local paper, telling Jenny how much I loved her. She did the same for me, which was a nice surprise. Then, on the morning of Valentine's Day, we heard a car repeatedly blaring its horn out in the car park and when we went to the windows there was Jenny. She'd taken the morning off work and bought at least a dozen helium heart-shaped balloons, which she'd tied to her wing mirrors, windscreen wipers, aerial and door handles. The gesture kept me smiling all day.

One of my jobs was to clean out the cells after the prisoners had vacated them. There was one inmate who seemed to be angry with everyone and would bang on his door for hours on end, spitting at us as we passed his cell en route to clean others. He stopped eating for a while and threw the bucket that he used as a toilet out into the corridor. We had to clean up all the spilled piss and the guards took his bucket away from him. He then started pissing under the door from inside the cell. We tried blocking the gap with towels, but then he started shitting in the cell and writing on the walls with it. The smell penetrated the whole floor.

Eventually he was taken down to B Wing (generally known as 'Beirut'), which was the only part of the prison that hadn't been modernised; the conditions were much the same as they'd been a hundred years before. This wing housed all the most violent prisoners and anyone who had been sent down for 'disruptive' behaviour. Half of the wing was cordoned off with a wooden wall, behind which were all the prisoners who were in for sexual offences. They were known as 'nonces' by other prisoners and were given a hard time.

We were all locked into our rooms while Mr Angry was being moved and we watched as six menacing looking officers in black riot gear and gloves opened his cell door and rushed in to overpower him. We could hear him yelling and fighting, even over the shouting of the guards and the banging and slamming of doors as they carried him, one on each thrashing limb and two holding his waist, away to his new home. Once he was safely out of the way we were given rubber gloves and told to scrub his shit off the walls. It was a struggle not to be sick as we worked. When we'd finished I stood under the showers until the smell had gone.

Frank left in March and we all moved up one bed. A twenty-one-year-old kid came in to take my place at the bottom of the pecking order. He was in for two years for causing death by dangerous driving. He had knocked over a lady who was out walking her dog. He got my job and I moved up to laundry duties, which gave me a lot more time to lie on the bed and read or think.

When Leslie the financial adviser left, he was replaced by Jimmy, who, I soon discovered, had attacked a friend of a friend of mine in a pub. The man had made a fool of Jimmy in front of his mates and so Jimmy got a foot-long blade and slashed him viciously. Realising he'd gone too far and that his victim was losing too much blood, he'd then driven the man to the hospital and dumped him in A&E. I decided to keep quiet about knowing the man.

I had pinned a picture of Sonia up in my locker and a lot of the guys said they fancied her. Tommy even asked if he could write to her as I'd told him she was having a hard time with Neil. She'd even had to take out an injunction against him to keep him away from the house after one weekend of particularly vicious beatings. Sonia did respond to Tommy's letter, but I could tell she was wary of any man who was inside, and in any case she and Neil soon got back together, despite the injunction, showing just how self-destructive her behaviour was.

The weather began to warm up in April, and we were allowed into a small yard where there was some grass that we could lie on and stare at the sky, imagining we were somewhere else. Jimmy and I started to get on quite well and often worked together. One night we were taking hot water and teabags round to the cells, talking and joking as we went. Jimmy was chatting to someone in one cell and I moved on to the next on my own, surprised that the prisoner, a slim Asian man, wasn't waiting for me at the door with his empty cup. I peered through the hatch to see if he was asleep. I couldn't see him on the bed and then I saw his feet hovering off the floor as if he were floating. It was a surreal moment and I couldn't make sense of it for a second.

Then I realised what had happened and jumped away from the door. I tried to shout but no sound came out of my mouth. I ran to fetch the guards and realised I was going in the opposite direction, my arms flapping about in panic while Jimmy tried in vain to kick the reinforced steel door in. I ran until I found two officers talking to a duty nurse. I still couldn't speak but they could tell from the look on my face and the way I was gesturing for them to follow me that something serious had happened.

'What's up?' one of them yelled, but I just kept running to where Jimmy was still trying to break through the door.

The first officer took one look through the hatch before finding the key and throwing the door open. He ran in with his colleague while the nurse tried to restrain Jimmy

'It's too late,' one of the officers said, 'he's gone.'

'No he's not!' Jimmy pushed past the nurse and got behind the hanging man, lifting him into the air to take the weight off the noose. 'Cut him down, quick!'

The nurse ran to get a blade of some sort and they got him down. We were told to go back to our cells and forget about the drinks round while an ambulance was called and he was taken to Leeds General Infirmary. Once things had calmed down the nurse came to check that Jimmy and I were all right and later that night we were told the Asian had survived. He came back the next day and was put on suicide watch with a nurse stationed outside his new cell, which had a gate rather than a solid door. A few days later in the exercise yard I saw him walking alone and asked him if he was OK. He thanked me for saving him.

'Why are you in here?' I asked.

'I drive a taxi,' he explained, 'and one night I picked up this prostitute for some business. When I'd finished with her she asked me for more money than we'd agreed. I said no and so she phoned the police and accused me of raping her. I just couldn't face the thought of years in prison.'

I couldn't think of anything to say to him.

Despite the payments Sonia had been making, the mortgage company was talking about repossessing my house unless I could prove I had a job to come out to. Dad's brother Dennis, who had a building firm, wrote promising a fictitious job, which seemed to quieten them down again, but I was still terrified they would change their minds and I wouldn't be able to do anything about it.

Around the end of May Jenny came to see me and I could tell something had changed between us. Our goodbye kiss was short and polite with none of the lingering passion of other visits. I sensed something was wrong and as I knew she was going back to Sonia's (they had become good friends), I gave her enough time to make the journey, then rang my sister.

'She thinks it's better if you don't talk,' Sonia told me, 'and just go your separate ways.'

It felt as if my world had come to an end. After hanging up the phone I couldn't do anything but stare into space in shock. I couldn't eat or read or sleep or joke with the others. After twenty-four hours of abject misery I asked if I could see a doctor. I told him what had happened and how it had made me feel.

'Don't you think your reaction is a little out of proportion for the time you and this young lady have been together?' he asked.

I nodded dumbly, knowing he was right, but it didn't make the pain any less real. As always I'd pinned all my hopes on one person, giving her an impossible emotional burden to carry so soon. For months I'd spent every second of every day thinking about Jenny and now it was over I was in mourning. I kept trying to ring her, but only got the answering machine. Tommy had warned me that it was bad to be in a relationship in prison. He told me he'd learned to end whatever relationship he was in as soon as he was sent away. The doctor gave me some tranquillisers to help me sleep.

With Jenny gone from my life I felt terribly lonely and started writing to two ex-girlfriends. I was desperate not to be on my own as I tried to restart my life. Both of them turned me down, knowing that I was contacting them for all the wrong reasons. Jenny must have heard about the letters and felt some jealousy because she came to visit me again and we discussed being friends when I came out.

'I don't like the thought of not having you in my life,' she told me.

I grabbed at this straw, even though I couldn't work out what she was thinking.

On my final day in prison I got up at dawn and gave away everything I didn't want to take out with me. It was July 1997 and I had served six months. An officer took me down to reception where I was held for an hour before my name was called. The box my belongings had been stored in was opened and my sad, crumpled clothes were pulled out. I changed and stepped out of the opened door of the prison.

Sonia was there. She was wearing a full-length fake leopard-skin coat and held a can of lager in one hand and two envelopes in the other. One was a card from Jenny saying she couldn't wait to see me and the other was a £400 tax rebate.

chapter sixteen
a suicide pact

I might have been out of jail but everything else about my life seemed hopeless. The initial rush of excitement at being free was soon drowned by the reality of my situation. I was now an ex-con, with no job and few prospects. I felt lonely and isolated and missed the companionship of my fellow prisoners. There seemed to be an awful lot of hours to fill in each day. And an awful lot of days stretching ahead.

Although the tax rebate was a nice surprise, it wasn't long before the money had run out. I was getting nowhere in my job search, so it looked like I was going to lose the house, and the thought of going back to the council blocks I had escaped from made me despair. Despite the card, everything seemed to be more or less over between me and Jenny, but we hadn't discussed the situation since I had been released. As always, talking to Sonia was one of my greatest comforts; she always understood how I was feeling because we both knew how it felt to have a bad memory so powerful that it caused you pain every single day of your life.

Her relationship with Neil had grown steadily worse as he became more possessive and abusive towards her. Leanne, Sonia's beautiful and adored child, was having to live with all the fighting and drinking, just as we had done. Sonia's drinking was completely out of control again and the thought of the damage she might be doing to Leanne on top of all the other pressures was breaking her heart.

'I've had enough,' I grumbled to her on the phone one Friday evening from the public phone box outside my house. 'Life just doesn't seem worth living any more.'

'I feel the same,' she agreed.

'Why don't we call it a day?' I suggested. 'End it once and for all?'

'At least then we'd be back with Mum,' she pointed out.

At that moment the idea of killing ourselves seemed perfectly reasonable, even though I hadn't formulated any sort of plan of how to do it. At least it would give me something to think about and a possible escape route from all my unhappiness, I thought. She said she was going to Leeds city centre on a pub crawl. Leanne was at her grandparents' house. I told her I was going to take the train to Halifax to see Jenny, then I hung up, feeling numb from everything that was going wrong.

Jenny and I had some tea together and avoided talking about our relationship, neither of us wanting to stir up an argument or cause any new agony, either for ourselves or for one another. I wanted to put off the final moments of the relationship for as long as possible, aware that the pain of a final parting would be even more intense than the dull ache I was already suffering. After eating we settled down in front of the television, preferring to stare passively at a screen rather than face up to the decisions we knew we had to take. The phone rang at around nine. It was Sonia for me. She sounded extremely drunk.

'I've taken my thirty paracetamol,' she informed me. 'So, are you going to join me?'

Suddenly the lethargic mood of the evening deserted me. 'Sonia, no!' I shouted. 'Stay where you are, don't go anywhere, please.'

I hung up and dialled 999, telling them what I'd just heard and giving them Sonia's address. My heart and mind were racing. Why was I in Halifax? I couldn't bear the thought that I was so far away from Leeds. I wanted to be there with my sister as she had so often been there for me. Jenny and I dithered around in an agony of indecision until, twenty minutes later, an ambulance man called me back to say he was at the house.

'She won't go to the hospital,' he told me, 'unless you're there with her. She's very drunk and aggressive.'

'OK,' I said. 'I'll get there as quickly as I can.'

Jenny agreed to drive me to Leeds. The eighteen-mile journey seemed to take for ever, every traffic light red, every driver slow. When I got there the ambulance was still parked outside and Sonia's front door was standing wide open. We ran in just in time to see Sonia stumbling downstairs towards us, her hair matted, her legs giving way beneath her. The living room was a mess, the furniture being knocked in every direction as Sonia staggered around the house, banging into things. I could see an empty tablet bottle lying amongst the discarded beer cans.

'Come on, Sonia,' I said, as authoritatively as I could manage, 'let's go.'

The ambulance men were telling us that we had to leave now, that the longer we delayed the more serious it would become, but Sonia wasn't being reasonable. She was refusing to leave the house and telling them loudly about her pact with me to end our lives together. I was embarrassed and ashamed to think that I'd contributed the spark that had led to this explosion. The thought of the drugs inside her, poisoning her system with every minute, was making me frantic.

The A&E department was crowded with injured people waiting for treatment. The nurse who saw Sonia explained that they would have to do some blood tests to see how much damage has been done before they could treat her. It was confirmed that she had indeed taken a dangerous dose. She was admitted, put to bed and given a drip.

Once she was safely asleep, Jenny took me home. I was too tired now to think about talking over the end of our relationship. But despite the tiredness I couldn't sleep as I lay in bed thinking about my sister and feeling desperately alone.

In the morning I rang Neil to tell him what had happened and to suggest that a hospital visit might be in order. I wanted the nursing staff to see that Sonia had people who cared about whether she lived or died, that she wasn't some hopeless case who wasn't worth saving. Even though they were always fighting, Neil was good at cheering her up when she was really down. By the time I got to the hospital at noon he was already there.

Sonia wasn't in her bed, having got up and wheeled her portable drip into a small sitting room near the ward where people were allowed to smoke. We sat chatting as if nothing had happened. Sonia's spirits seemed high, as if she realised she'd made a mistake, and I left her for the rest of the day, feeling much relieved.

Neil stayed for a while, then went out into Leeds for the night with some friends. At 1 a.m. he reappeared at the hospital and Sonia told me what happened the next day.

He was obviously strung out on something, probably a mixture of cocaine, Ecstasy and speed. He managed to get past the nurses' station without being noticed and tried to get into Sonia's bed. She ordered him to pack it in and the rejection stoked his aggression. As the nurse approached, Sonia decided the wisest decision would be to get out of the bed herself, ushering Neil – who was now rolling a joint – back into the little sitting room before he disturbed all the other patients. Those in beds close by had already been woken.

A security officer arrived and asked Neil to leave. Neil stood up, puffing his joint defiantly, and hurled abuse at the man, who promptly radioed for help. Neil barged past the man and brushed away the nurses who tried to stop him getting back into the ward. Sonia realised that she had no choice but to get him out of the hospital as quickly as possible before he hit someone. All the other patients were awake now. She called over a nurse and asked her to take the tube out of her arm.

'You shouldn't do that,' the nurse warned. 'You really need to wait till the morning until you've had the full course.'

'Get this bloody thing off me!' Sonia screamed, and the nurse took out her scissors, cutting through the tube a couple of inches away from where the needle went into her arm.

Sonia then hustled Neil out of the ward, stripping away the surgical tape on her arm and pulling the needle out, dropping it into an ashtray as she went. Outside the hospital, for whatever reason, Neil picked up a discarded bottle and hurled it to the ground, smashing it to pieces, just as a police car rounded the corner, no doubt summoned by the security guards. Two officers got out of the car and Neil calmed down. Bullying hospital security guards was one thing, policemen quite another. They drove him away in handcuffs.

Sonia ordered a taxi to take her home, where she changed into a comfortable tracksuit and contemplated what she should do next. The house was cold, dark and lonely and she made a small effort to tidy it up, but it didn't make things seem any better. She made herself a cup of tea and eventually fell asleep.

At around five o'clock she was woken by the sound of a car door slamming and she knew Neil had returned even before he started banging on the door and shouting her name. The moment she opened the door to quieten him down he grabbed her by the throat and propelled her back into the house, yelling at her that it was all her fault he'd been arrested. She managed to break free and ran out into the street, screaming for help, with him close behind. He caught up with her a few houses down the street, grabbing her tracksuit top as she struggled in vain to get away from his grip. A car turned into the street and she managed to get free long enough to run in front of it, forcing the driver to screech to a halt. The man behind the wheel jumped out to help her, and then realised that he knew Neil. The two men talked about old times for a few moments and then, extraordinarily, the man drove away. Neil grabbed Sonia's top again, trying to drag her back to the house and, as she wriggled to be free, it came off over her head, leaving her naked to the waist. Sonia fully appreciated the danger she was in and thought she was about to be killed, just like mum.

Confident that Sonia was now powerless, Neil turned, with her top in his hand like a trophy, and walked back into the house, ordering her to follow. Sonia stood in the street half naked, crying and not knowing what to do next.

Then a door opened in one of the other houses and a young

man beckoned to her. Sonia glanced quickly at Neil's departing back and darted into the man's house before Neil could turn round and see where she was going. Once she was inside, another young man and a woman threw a blanket round her. They looked like students and she guessed they must have been watching the whole scene. She was deeply grateful for their courage. Between uncontrollable sobs she told them what had happened.

They phoned the police who arrived a few minutes later. When they realised that Neil was the same man they'd picked up a few hours before they called for back-up and two more cars arrived. Neil came out of the door, shouting, and five of the officers pounced on him before he could do anything, while the sixth one stayed in the car with Sonia.

As Neil was led past the cars to the van, he leaned down, stared in at Sonia and screamed, 'Bitch!'

'Is there anywhere we can take you so you don't have to spend the rest of the night on your own?' the policeman enquired, and Sonia asked them to take her to Angela's house.

Angela had been drinking all night when they got there and was out cold, so Sonia let herself in and waited. When Angela eventually woke at eleven the next morning they drove to the local Liberal Club, where they knew they would find Dad. Sonia sat silently in the corner of the club drinking orange juice, trying to work out what she should do with her life now.

Of course Neil worked out where they were, and when he arrived, exploding with abuse, the whole club fell silent. The police, it seemed, had not been able to charge him with anything. They had probably hoped to calm the situation by removing him for a few hours at a time.

Now he wore no top, and his muscles were pumped up like a wrestler's. He seemed to have lost all powers of reason and no one wanted to interfere with him, except an off-duty policeman, who was having a drink in the club and decided he'd heard enough. He stood up to tell Neil who he was.

'I don't care who you fucking are,' Neil snarled. 'If you don't sit down I'll stick my hand into your stomach and pull out your liver.'

Angela had bravely slipped to the toilet and phoned the police, and the first Neil knew about this was when he spotted two police cars drawing up outside the window. He ran outside, presumably so they wouldn't be able to get him into a corner. He was backing away from the cars to the other end of the street, but they'd obviously called for more support and another car arrived, cutting off his escape route. The police were asking him to calm down and come quietly, but he was still screaming and shouting that he hadn't done anything wrong.

This was the moment when I arrived in the street to be confronted by what looked like a scene from a Rambo movie. A crowd had formed, everybody wanting to see what happened next, and a police van moved in to the end of the street.

'What the hell's going on, Neil?' I asked.

'Richard,' he pleaded, 'tell them I'm OK.'

For a second he sounded like a little boy asking for help, and at that moment the police leaped on him, handcuffed him once more and threw him into the van.

Dad, Sonia and Angela came out of the club then and we all headed for the pub opposite. We got in a round of drinks and I could see Sonia was badly shaken. As she filled me in on the night's events, Neil's friends came into the pub. We expected the tables to start flying and people to get hurt, but they didn't seem to be looking for a fight. One of them came over to me and shook my hand. 'I hear you've just come out,' he said. 'Are you OK?'

It seemed that having served time gave me some sort of badge of honour. He asked what Neil had been up to and we explained as if we were all talking about a naughty schoolboy. I realised I was growing tired of the whole culture of the place: a culture that allowed a man to drive away from a woman who was obviously in danger, a culture in which men thought of prison as being no more than an inconvenience. I didn't want to become one of these people who spent every day sitting in pubs and clubs, or whose only idea of a good time was to get drunk and pick a fight.

For the next few days I spent a lot of time with Sonia, making sure she didn't do anything else stupid. She was still drinking and at times I drank with her, because it seemed like the only thing to do. I felt I'd played a part in the disaster of that night and I knew that I had to do something to sort our family situation out, otherwise we were going to go on like this for ever, until we ended up killing ourselves and one another.

chapter seventeen
turning it round

Once my relationship with Jenny was finally and painfully over, I returning to bouncing from one girl to another. I was still desperate to have a steady girlfriend, but until that happened I craved physical comfort with any women who were willing to provide it. Many of them were totally unsuitable and the relationships died before they even got started, and every time I met someone nice I ended up spoiling it by becoming insecure and certain that they were about to dump me.

I was desperately in need of money and was visiting the job club for ex-convicts every day, increasingly worried that I would lose my house if I didn't find some way of meeting the payments soon. The idea of having the house taken away was unbearable. It was the only thing that stood between me and the sort of squalid life that Dad and Sonia lived. It was my sanctuary and my stepping-stone to a better life. If that went I would have nothing left.

Then, two days before the mortgage company's final deadline for repossessing the house, just as I was giving up all hope, I spotted a small ad in the *Yorkshire Post* for a warehouse supervisor for a fashion company. I'd worked with my previous company for almost five years and knew everything there was to know about warehousing and distribution. It seemed well worth a go.

I called the number and the agency asked me down for an informal interview. I went home for a shirt and tie and returned to the city centre, knowing that this was probably my last chance at finding a job before I lost my beloved house and slid off the housing ladder, possibly for ever. Maybe, I thought, if I could get a promise of a job the mortgage company would give me an extension, although even that was an outside chance now. I popped in to see Sonia on the way and she gave me a mock interview to try to overcome my nerves. She assured me I'd be fine and I left for the real thing, muttering prayers under my breath, hardly daring to imagine the consequences for my life if I failed.

The interviewer at the agency was happy with me and rang the employer to say they had someone good for the job. If they'd offered me an interview the following week it would have been too late to save the house, but they said to come round there and then. I hardly dared breathe; I was still in with a final chance.

The agency interviewer drove me to the company, which was located close to the Room at the Top where Mum had enjoyed her last drink on the night she was killed, and where I'd been picked up by the Middleton landlord. I thought about the coincidence and about Mum as I sat in reception, while the agency interviewer went in to talk about me with the boss. My stomach was churning. Then a small, casually dressed man called Lawrence came out and asked me a few questions about my previous job. The fashion business in Leeds is a small world and we knew several of the same people. He took me on a tour of the premises. The company supplied high street stores with ladieswear. There were garments strewn everywhere and only a few young lads in the warehouse. I was sure I could do the job if I was given the chance.

'When could you start if we wanted to offer you the job?' he asked once we were back in the office.

'Immediately,' I said.

'Why did you leave your last job?' he asked.

'My dad was taken ill,' I lied. 'So I took off some time to look after him.'

'You've never been in trouble with the police, have you?' he asked. My stomach muscles tightened and my mouth went dry. I had a choice: I could tell the truth and almost certainly lose the opportunity; or I could lie and get the job. I hated the fact that I had reached a stage where I was forced to make such a choice.

'No,' I lied, hoping I wasn't blushing or giving myself away.

At the end of the interview I was told I could start the following Monday.

I left, feeling as though I was floating on air. I'd done it. Just when I thought I couldn't turn the situation round, I had. I went back to court and with the help of a man from the Citizens Advice Bureau I put together a repayment plan to pay off the mortgage, which they accepted. My next step was to find a way to pay off my bank and credit card debts, which had grown to about £4,000. One job wasn't going to be enough and so I got a weekend job in a nightclub as well to earn some extra cash. It looked just possible that I'd found a way out of a very black hole.

The plan was for me to learn the ropes at the warehouse and then take over from the supervisor, which created a bit of an atmosphere. After my first week Adrian, the production manager, came back from holiday. He was a lot tougher than Lawrence and I wondered if he would have given me the job so easily. I lived in fear of him finding me out and giving me my cards. Instead, I was promoted to be his assistant. I was exultant, but still couldn't feel safe.

Eager to pay my debts off as quickly as possible, I went on working weekends at the club, until someone recognised me and the management made up a reason to get rid of me. I joined the telesales staff at the *Yorkshire Post*, which paid twice as much.

In December that year, another ad in the paper caught my eye: 'Would Sonia McCann or her brother or sister or anyone knowing of their whereabouts contact this box number ASAP.'

I knew it was to do with our past because for years Sonia had been using Mum's maiden name, as Mum and Dad hadn't been married when she was born. I sent a letter to the box number and awaited a reply. Eventually I got a call. A woman explained, in a very soothing voice, that she was a television researcher and that she had read about Sonia and me going out looking for Mum on the morning after she was murdered. She said she thought it would make a good TV drama. I went to see Sonia as soon as I'd finished work. Neither of us felt comfortable about the idea and I was terrified that if there was any publicity about us the people at work would find out I'd been to prison. We eventually told her we didn't want to go ahead.

After three months assisting Adrian, I plucked up my courage and asked the director for a rise. To my surprise he told me I could have another £30 a week. I couldn't believe it. I'd managed to make a success of my job, and that made me very proud. I knew my bosses valued me and I loved going in to work. Even when we shut down for Christmas I couldn't wait to get back there. I didn't have a job title, but I knew I was as close to indispensable as anyone can ever get, my office always full of people asking for information and streams of e-mails always coming in.

My main job was ordering fabric and arranging for its delivery to wherever the garments were going to be made. To begin with we used British suppliers, but like many other companies we'd started moving production to Sri Lanka in order to cut costs. From the moment I arrived in the office to the moment I left I would be busy, always doing two or three different things at once, and I loved the buzz.

I was enjoying myself so much I was terrified that they would find out about my past and it would all be over. I became paranoid about everything. I would believe I saw a look in the director's eye or I would overhear someone whispering into a phone and be convinced they were talking about me. If I bumped into someone in the street that I knew from the past and they asked me where I was working I wouldn't tell them, not wanting to take the risk of them informing on me. Chance meetings like this would throw me into a panic and I would have to get a drink of water as quickly as possible because my mouth would go dry with fear. I was absolutely petrified of losing my job and getting back onto the downward slide.

I also enjoyed the work at the *Yorkshire Post* and made some good friends, particularly a girl called Karen who was to become my best friend and play a major part in helping me to turn my life around. She was the most alive and exciting person I'd ever met, a mixed-race girl and a budding actress. We laughed all the time and found we could tell each other anything.

I was equally paranoid about the *Yorkshire Post* finding out about my past because as well as liking the job, I was just beginning to get my finances straight. When they organised a sponsored abseil down the side of the building, with a photo shoot afterwards, I was all for it, carried along on the adrenalin of the event. But as I walked home afterwards, a wave of anxiety swept over me with the realisation that my name and face were now going to be appearing in the *Yorkshire Post*, which someone might spot and tip the paper off about my past.

At the same time I was sane enough to realise that my fears of being exposed and of losing everything I had worked for were driving me crazy and that I had to do something about them if I wasn't going to be living on my nerves for the rest of my life; so I decided to go to a hypnotherapist for help. I knew the problem was inside my mind and I wanted to find someone who could change the way I thought. I found one quite close to the office and was rather looking forward to the experience once I'd plucked up the courage to make an appointment. A young woman answered the door and invited me in. It felt good to be able to unburden all my fears and feelings onto her; to be able to talk freely about the things that I had to keep hidden from almost everyone else. I kept going back to her each week and we tried various different exercises, some of which involved hypnotism, which felt just like being very relaxed and able to explore my own imagination.

She would ask me to visualise different scenes from my life and on one occasion she asked me to remember one of my happiest moments. I pictured the time when I was sitting on Mum's knee in the hospital corridor, having banged my head on the bed, and I tried to hang on to the feeling for as long as possible. The glow of happiness lasted for a couple of days after that.

Although I enjoyed the sessions and was gaining confidence, the anxiety attacks and paranoia were not going away. I knew I was lucky in many ways now. I had a good job, a steady income and a nice house. But I also knew that all of it would mean nothing if our family life went on lurching from one disaster to the next. My success seemed so precarious, as if it could be swept away at any moment by some new drama beyond my control.

I was managing to cling on to my home, my job and my sanity, but Sonia was continuing to get into one mess after another and one night, just before Christmas 2000, she disappeared. No one knew where she was. I didn't worry too much, assuming that she'd gone on a bender or found a new boyfriend, and when Angela eventually rang on Christmas Eve to tell me Sonia had called to say she was on her way home I went round to see her. There was no light or heat on in the house when I got there because Sonia had lost her token for the electricity meter; she was always losing her handbags with her money, phone and cards in. I found her lying on the sofa in the silent, chilly gloom, looking disgusting, with Leanne sitting forlornly beside her. She seemed hardly able to move. I rummaged round the kitchen, looking for something to feed her, but she obviously had no food in at all.

Leanne was due to be picked up by Andy and it was clear that Sonia couldn't spend Christmas with his family, so I called a cab to take her over to my place once Leanne had gone. Because she'd eaten nothing for days, just surviving on beer, she could hardly move without being sick but we eventually got back. I had to ask the driver to stop on the way for Sonia to throw up.

I settled her down on the sofa with a quilt and made her some tomato soup, having rushed out to the supermarket to get the tomatoes, onions, garlic and cream that I needed for the recipe. She laughed at me for my domestic skills, but she still enjoyed the meal. We watched all the Christmas programmes together and it was nice looking after her. Leanne's granddad brought her over on Christmas Day and we spent a few pleasant hours together.

In the New Year, things continued getting better for me. There was an awards ceremony each year at the *Yorkshire Post* and one of my supervisors suggested that it might be worth my while attending. I didn't pick up on her hint and stayed away. When I walked into work the following Friday everyone started applauding and I discovered I'd won the Best Telesales Canvasser of the year. I felt wonderful.

Sonia took to ringing me in the middle of the night, having had too much to drink, and telling me how much she loved me. I didn't appreciate having my sleep disturbed all the time when I had to get up for work, especially as I would then find myself lying awake and worrying about her. I wanted her to be able to get some pleasure from her life, as I was now doing, but I couldn't work out how to help her.

One weekend she disappeared again, leaving Leanne alone in the house. Leanne, who was being forced to become an adult as fast as Sonia herself had had to, made her own way over to Angela's house when it became obvious her mother wasn't coming home. Sonia didn't reappear for two weeks and after a few days Leanne went to her grandparents, deciding this time to stay with them. Sonia had lost her daughter. I felt so sorry for Leanne because although Sonia was still alive, she was having to grow up without her mother around and I knew how that felt.

Later in that year, Sonia met her next boyfriend Jed, who had spotted her through a pub window. Jed wore his ginger hair closely cropped to disguise the fact that it was thinning and both his heavily freckled, hairy arms sported tattoos. Although I was relieved to see the back of Neil, I didn't think Jed was much of an improvement and he didn't like my relationship with Sonia one bit. When he heard once that Sonia and I had been to the cinema together he couldn't understand it. Why would a brother and sister go out together? The only answer, he decided, was that we had a sexual relationship of some sort.

Despite the battering she'd given her system, Sonia looked several years younger than thirty-three and many men still fancied her. She had lovely, long, brown hair, which was always in good condition, despite the fact that she'd never set foot in a hairdresser's since Dad had attacked her hair with wallpapering scissors many years before. She could have done so much better but she seemed to be irresistibly attracted to possessive, manipulative men with a violent streak. Because she was heavily in debt to loan sharks, Sonia was forced to move in with Jed to escape their attentions, even though her gut instincts, like mine, told her that it was going to be a mistake.

One afternoon she went out drinking and visited another man

that she knew. They went for a drive south and she was drinking all the way. There was always a point during Sonia's drinking when she would turn nasty, just like Dad. I could always see that moment coming and was able to take evasive action in the way I spoke to her; other men didn't necessarily see the danger signals in time. Inevitably she rowed with this man in the car and he dumped her beside the motorway in the middle of nowhere.

Despite her inebriated state she got herself to a service station and tried picking up another guy in the hope he would take her home. Everything after that was a bit of a blur and when she eventually came round she felt as though the man had had sex with her and felt used. She asked the guy to take her home and he said he just had to go and get his car. He drove off in the van, telling her to wait there beside the road for him. When she finally realised he wasn't coming back she approached a young woman.

'Which way is it to Leeds city centre?' Sonia asked.

'Leeds?' The woman looked surprised. 'This is Leicester, love.'

It was about six in the evening by then. She eventually managed to find a phone box and called me, sobbing and begging me to come and get her. There was no way the old Ford Escort I'd recently bought would make a trip like that. I called her back in the box when her money ran out, trying to keep her calm so that she didn't storm off, since I would then have no idea how to find her.

'Give me five minutes to think what to do,' I said. 'Stay by the phone.'

As I hung up I screamed out loud. Why did these things have to keep happening? Sonia had got herself into exactly the sort of position that Mum was in on the night she died. I rang the police and got put through to a station near Leicester. I explained that my sister had been dumped by a motorway and had no way of getting home. They said they would go and pick her up.

I rang her back and kept her talking for fifteen minutes until they arrived and she hung up drunkenly. Fifteen minutes later the police rang to say she was OK and having a cup of tea.

'The last train's leaving Leicester for Leeds in twenty minutes,' the officer told me. 'If she misses that one there aren't any tomorrow because it's a bank holiday. If you can get to your local police station with twenty-five pounds we'll buy the ticket for her.'

I then had to race down to the police station in my old banger, grabbing a few notes off the coffee table as I went, with one eye on the clock. Within a few minutes I realised I was never going to make it to Leeds police station in time. Then I remembered there was a small station in a suburb nearby and made a quick detour, arriving seven minutes before the train was due to leave Leicester. I ran towards the door and banged into it with all my strength, but it didn't open and I was left shaking from the impact. The station was locked and there was now no way I could get to another one. I felt I'd let Sonia down. As I walked away I spotted a yellow emergency phone on the wall. I picked it up and told the woman my predicament. At that moment Sonia was being driven through Leicester at full speed towards the train station with the sirens blaring and lights flashing.

'Stay where you are,' the woman instructed me and two minutes later I could hear sirens approaching as another patrol car came racing to a halt beside me and an officer jumped out.

'Do you have something for me?' he demanded, and I handed over the money. He took out his radio and the message went through. Sonia was bought her ticket and packed onto the train with seconds to spare.

As I made my way back home, to return to whatever I was doing before her call came through, I wondered if I would ever be able to lead a normal life.

When I was promoted to supervisor at the *Yorkshire Post* it was suggested that I might benefit from attending an assertiveness course and I enrolled at a local college. I was aware that although my confidence was starting to build it was still paper-thin. The teacher was a woman called Sandra and I soon realised that the other people in the class all had fears of their own and that I wasn't alone. I enjoyed the classes, learning how to say 'no', how not to allow myself to lose control when things went wrong, how to relax, how to deal with anxiety and how to use breathing exercises. I learned how to ask for things without feeling like a child. I wished I'd done something like this years earlier.

chapter eighteen

deciding to survive

In 2000 an ITV company approached me and the girls about participating in a drama about the Yorkshire Ripper. We declined, but they very kindly invited us to a private viewing before it was screened. I went with Sonia and Donna. We sat in a small room, laid out like a cinema with four rows of chairs and a large television. They left us alone and we sat in silence as we were pulled back through a time warp to the event, twenty-five years earlier, that had changed our lives so completely. I wondered if viewers would give a second thought to the effects that night had had on us, or would think about how we might be feeling now. I knew Dad couldn't understand what the problem was, believing we should have got over it long ago. I had tried discussing such things with him so many times but he had just brushed my words aside. But then it was different for him. He was already separated from Mum by then. He didn't lose his mother. He seemed to be able to cut people out of his life without a second thought. These days he even ignored Pauline and his other children. But I still sometimes felt painful pangs of jealousy when I saw other people doing things with their mothers. The pain was there every day and probably always would be, although sometimes it was dangerously easy to deaden it with drink.

Sonia's relationship with Jed was becoming as difficult as the one with Neil had been. She was used to his ways by now: how he would only allow one side of their toast to be cooked as it saved money, how he would insist on only one television being on in the house to keep the electricity bill down and would never allow the heating to be turned on, telling Sonia to wear a fleece if she complained about the cold, how he locked the front door and wouldn't tell her where the key was.

One morning after a long night of drinking and arguing and violence, Jed clumsily tried to make amends. It didn't work and eventually he went off to the pub. That afternoon, once more the worse for wear, he managed to get Sonia to agree to sex, which she did in order to get some peace. It was quick and painful for her and as they lay beside each other afterwards the arguing started again. Sonia answered him back, making him angrier, and things got physical and nasty.

Jed started shouting at her and she ran out of the bedroom, banging against the bare walls of the corridor as she went, diving into the kitchen. She could hear his heavy breathing just behind her. She saw the knife she'd been using to peel potatoes for their lunch sitting beside the sink, and she snatched it up and spun round to face him. She didn't stop to think what she was doing, just stabbed him with a downward motion towards the heart. His face went white and blood started to drip from the hole she'd made in his chest, seeping like a nosebleed.

'What've you done?' he screamed, stumbling out and across to the living room, collapsing into the first chair.

Sonia, still naked, sank onto the sofa and just looked at him for a while. Then she walked back to the bedroom, picked up the phone and called an ambulance, getting dressed while they waited for it to arrive. The police were the first to get there, knocking on the door.

'Where's the fucking key?' she asked.

'Under the pillow,' he replied.

She let them in.

'I don't want to press charges,' Jed said as soon as he saw them.

'I did it,' she told them. 'I stabbed him.'

The police attended to Jed and then got out the handcuffs, informing Sonia they would have to take her to the station.

'There's no need for those,' she told them.

'I said I didn't want to press charges,' Jed repeated.

'It's a little too late for that, I'm afraid, son,' the policeman said.

David, who lived with Angela, rang me the next day at work to tell me what had happened. For years I'd been dreading getting a call that would inform me Sonia had been found dead, just like Mum, so this was almost more of a shock. By this time the police had already released her. When I told my boss at the office what had happened he told me to take as long as I needed to sort her out. As I steered my car out of the company forecourt and onto the road, fumbling with my seatbelt, tears came to my eyes. I knew what prison was like and I didn't think Sonia would be able to handle it.

In the end she was charged with ABH – Actual Bodily Harm – but the charges were dropped, as they were not deemed to be in the public interest.

Sonia stabbing Jed made me even more aware of just what a tightrope we were walking. Sonia had to straighten herself out, or yet another generation of our family would end up destroyed by drink and abusive relationships. So many times I had seen Sonia behaving in ways I was sure Mum must have behaved when she was that age and the possible consequences made me cold with fear.

I felt more despair that anger. The incident made me all the more determined to do something to save her before it was too late. I had to find a way to help her, to show her that there was another, better life possible if you just made the effort, if you just made the decision to survive.

At the same time as working for a living and looking after myself and my house, I was also seeking out new hobbies that would keep me away from the pubs and the clubs and the destructive behaviour patterns of my past. I took up mountain biking, and my best friend, Karen, introduced me to the wonders of salsa dancing, something that the men in my family would traditionally have scoffed at. I loved dancing, but this was very different from anything I'd experienced on the club scene. No one was on speed or Ecstasy and the atmosphere was so friendly I could walk up to anyone and chat without any fear of rejection. I could never imagine Dad in a place like this in a hundred years.

I began to feel truly well for the first time, stronger and more able to see what should be done to lead a better life. I booked myself onto a salsa holiday to Barcelona, and was nervous about the whole trip to begin with, particularly about eating out, as I was worried that I would get the etiquette wrong; I didn't even feel comfortable putting a napkin on my lap. But as the week went on my shyness melted away and it began to dawn on me that life could actually be great. There were about seventy-five of us and we would do a two-hour class every afternoon. Everyone who walked past the hotel would stop and watch us dancing in the sun with the music belting out.

The moment I got home I drove down to the photo processing company and had my three films developed while I waited, impatient to be able to relive the memories immediately, making the experience last a little longer. I showed them to everyone, wanting them to see that I was normal and getting on with my life.

When my assertiveness course ended, I asked the teacher, Sandra, if I could have a word with her in private. I explained that although I'd benefited from the classes I still had problems that we hadn't touched on. I couldn't go into everything there and then but I said how I was failing in relationships because I always expected women to leave me.

'It sounds like you could do with some counselling,' she said.

'Can you recommend someone good?' I asked.

'Actually I'm a trained counsellor,' she said. 'I'd be very happy to discuss things further if you want.'

I was comfortable with the idea of talking to someone I already knew and liked and so I made a date to meet her at her house. The room she took me to on the first day I turned up was warm and clean and relaxing and I tried to imagine what it would be like to be brought up in such a pleasant environment. Over the coming weeks I poured out everything and we discussed how people should behave in relationships. I told her what had happened with the man in the Middleton pub all those years ago, and she convinced me I wasn't responsible. She taught me about things like projection and how it had been allowing me to turn my worst fears into self-fulfilling prophecies. When I told her about incidents like Dad almost drowning me in the bath she explained to me how a loving father should have handled that situation, describing concepts of loving guidance that were completely unfamiliar to me.

She convinced me that I no longer needed to work seven days a week as I had now paid off my debts and was only doing two jobs because I was frightened of losing one. I gave in my notice at the *Yorkshire Post*, feeling ready to start living a normal life. For the first time ever I felt I was standing on solid ground and that I could now walk confidently towards whatever the future might hold for me.

The stabbing incident seemed to have shocked Sonia and made her determined to improve her life as well, although she had an even steeper hill to climb than I did. She spent some time in a women's shelter and then moved into sheltered housing for people who were trying to sort their lives out. It was run by the church and she had a room just big enough for a single bed and a chair. I took her and her few black sacks of possessions there on the first day because, as always, I wanted them to see that she had someone who cared for her. Leanne went to visit her there but Sonia was obviously embarrassed to be seen in such a place by her sixteen-year-old daughter. She was still drinking but not all the time, which was an improvement. She even had a job in a charity shop.

She came for an interview at my company and got a job working alongside me, just the two of us in the same office, fighting the situation together like we always had. I would pick her up and bring her in to work every morning to ensure she got there, but sometimes she was so heavily hungover from the night before she could hardly function and I had to cover up for her all day. She started drinking again at lunchtimes to deal with the pressure of the workplace and I cringed when I listened to her dealing with people on the phone, her confidence obviously fortified with beer. I tried talking to her about it but she just became angry and defensive.

Eventually she came back from the pub one day so obviously drunk that I had to tell her it couldn't go on. She stormed off and didn't return. I was sad she couldn't see how the money from the job could help her get her life together, but at the same time I was envious of her for having the balls to walk out of the place when I didn't. Although I had been so grateful for the job at the beginning, I was now finding the constant pressure and aggressive management style of the company difficult to live with, but I had to stay there because I wanted to keep my house. Like most of the world, I had got myself onto a treadmill.

Sonia eventually got her own place again, a two-bedroom house close to Angela's. She had nothing to furnish it with so I went out and bought myself a new sofa so I could give her my old one, bought her a double bed and decorated her bedroom. She started seeing Jed again, telling me that although he had his faults it was better than being alone, and I knew there was little chance of her meeting anyone better as long as she was still drinking. I'd been in enough unsuitable relationships myself over the years to know that sometimes you just needed to fill a gap in your life. There had always been a gap in our lives since Mum had gone.

As I racked my brain for ways in which Sonia and I could exorcise the demons of our past, the idea of writing this book began to dawn on me. I wanted to make my family's voices heard for once. Everyone else got to talk in the papers and in books about how their lives had been destroyed by the actions of Peter Sutcliffe and I wanted people to know how he had affected us; how the ripples were still travelling out across the pond nearly thirty years after he made the cruel decision to murder our mother, making us different from other people and changing some of the ways in which we led our lives. I wanted people to know that the pain of such an event never went away for long.

Sandra told me she thought I'd got as far as I could with counselling and that I was now ready to go out into the world on my own. I asked her what she thought about the idea of writing a book and she was very encouraging, assuring me that I shouldn't feel ashamed of anything I'd done and that it would help to get it all out onto paper.

I wanted to talk to Sonia about our lives together, to remind myself of some of the things we'd been through and to find out what it had been like for her, but her drinking was getting worse again and it was often hard to get sense out of her. She made another attempt at suicide, ending up in the psychiatric ward of the local hospital.

I refused to believe I couldn't reclaim my and my sisters' self-respect. I knew we weren't going to find it in a bottle or a club, but books had helped me in prison and I believed that words could help me again now. I joined the Leeds Writers' Circle to try to find people who would be able to guide me and tell me if I was on the right lines. At the first meeting I read out the synopsis I'd prepared with agonising care. When I finished reading there was a terrible, shocked silence as the rest of the group tried to think of something to say to me. It was uncomfortable for all of us and for a few seconds I wished I'd never started on the project, but I knew I was going to have to get used to people knowing about my past if I was going to go through with it. When they found the words the other group members all assured me that my story should be told.

At a later meeting a guest speaker who was a teacher of writing advised me not to go through the agony of writing the whole thing but to send the synopsis to some literary agents and I took his advice, receiving a positive response. I felt excited that things were moving forward, but frightened at the thought of exposing our lives to the rest of the world after so many years of covering up and keeping secrets. Writing the book helped me to see what was important and gave me the courage to walk away from the job I wasn't enjoying any more and find another one.

At the end of July I got a call from Sonia. She was drunk and saying that she'd had enough and wanted to go back to the security of the psychiatric ward in the hospital where she had been taken after her last suicide attempt. When I got to her house she was walking round and round in circles, very fast, muttering unintelligible things. I sat her down and tried to calm her.

'I've lost my mind, Richard,' she told me.

'You can lose your mind if you want to,' I said, 'just as long as you keep a little room at the back where everything is OK.'

'There is a little room where everything is normal,' she assured me, 'but the shutters are coming down.'

'You'd better find something to stop them, then,' I warned, and she smiled.

I took her down to A&E and the doctor there suggested he book her onto a detox programme. She started a few weeks later, determined at last to stop drinking, afraid that the alcohol was finally stealing her sanity.

The programme began to have an effect and as her mind cleared we spent more time retracing everything that had happened in our lives together. There were things she'd never told me before, which now came bubbling to the surface, some of them heartbreaking, but all of them helping to cement the bond that has always been there between us. She told me, for the first time, that Keith, Mum's boyfriend, had raped her when she was a small child. I was horrified.

'I know you've seen me and your mum do it,' he told her the first time, 'so you do the same. Your mum knows all about this;

it's no good going to her with tales.'

Sonia told me how he wanted to do it to Donna as well but Sonia made so much fuss he gave up trying and carried on satisfying himself with her. She believed that by giving in to his desires and keeping quiet she might be able to save the other girls, who she thought were too small to be able to cope with the physical pain. She believed it was her responsibility to protect the rest of us. She remembered that sometimes Mum changed her bed to face the window and she could watch the stars while Keith was doing his thing to her, imagining she was up there instead.

I chose the literary agent that I liked the best and on the day we met in London for lunch my grandma in Inverness died. A week later I went up to Scotland with Donna, to represent Mum at the funeral. Although it was a sad occasion and it was horrible to see Mum's ten brothers and sisters in so much pain, I felt happy to be seeing everyone again for the first time since Sonia and I had been up there as teenagers. I guess that, for my aunts and uncles, seeing us brought back memories of their own childhoods, reminding them of their lost mother and sister and all the pain there had been through the years. I'm sure they had happy memories too, which must have made the reminder of their loss even sharper.

Everyone fussed around us from the moment we arrived and it actually felt like we had a family that cared for us at last. I was more able to talk to them now that I had come to terms with the damage of the past. I finally felt that I had become a normal person, that I could care for my other family members as an equal, and the feeling brought me close to them after being so distant for so long.

In the church everyone was crying from the moment the organ started playing, but my eyes remained stubbornly dry. I felt as though I was observing it all from the outside. Then the vicar started talking about the woman who had brought Mum into the world and his words struck me powerfully. I realised he was talking about where I had come from, about the women who had created me. He spoke about how respected and loved my grandmother was by all who knew her.

'Now Betsy is with her husband and her daughter, Wilma,' he said, and instantly the tears came up from inside my chest like a tidal wave.

I fought painfully to maintain my self-control. Had my grandma felt the same pain every day since Mum's death? I remembered the night Sonia and I had gone out hand in hand into the early morning mist looking for our mother, and the visit I'd paid to her grave on my own. As the images came back to me, my sobbing swelled out of control, making my chest and throat ache.

Not having been to Mum's funeral, I felt I was finally saying goodbye to her.

I cried as if all the pain I had been holding in for a quarter of a century was being released at last.

For further information about Richard and a preview
of his next book *Into the Light* go to his website:

www.richardmccann.co.uk

SAMM (Support After Murder and Manslaughter)

Registered Charity No: 1000598

Cranmer House

39 Brixton Road

London SW9 6DZ

020 7735 3838

www.samm.org.uk

SAMARITANS

Registered Charity No: 219432

Tel: 08457 90 90 90 (24 Hours).

www.samaritans.org